WELCOMING THE CHRIST CHILD WITH PADRE PIO

"Padre Pio's love of Christmas, devotion to Christ, and childlike innocence as shared in *Welcoming the Christ Child with Padre Pio* provide us with an excellent guide for a prayerful Advent through daily quotes, fascinating stories, seasonal scriptures, and personal reflection. This book is a true gift for your Advent!"

Allison Gingras
Host and creator of the podcast *A Seeking Heart*

"Padre Pio loved Christmas, and Susan De Bartoli's book takes us beautifully through Advent with him. De Bartoli shares her deep love and knowledge of, and devotion to, Padre Pio in stories, reflections, and prayers as we go through each day of the season. *Welcoming the Christ Child with Padre Pio* is a unique and special way to celebrate the Christmas season with Padre Pio."

Julie Fitts Ritter
Executive director of the Padre Pio Foundation of America

WELCOMING THE CHRIST CHILD WITH PADRE PIO

Daily Reflections for Advent

SUSAN DE BARTOLI

AVE MARIA PRESS AVE Notre Dame, Indiana

Nihil Obstat: Reverend Monsignor Michael Heintz, PhD
                   Censor Librorum

Imprimatur: Most Reverend Kevin C. Rhoades
                 Bishop of Fort Wayne–South Bend

Given at: Fort Wayne, Indiana, on 18 March 2022

Founded in 1865, Ave Maria Press is a ministry of the United States Province of Holy Cross.

www.avemariapress.com

Paperback: ISBN-13 978-1-64680-172-5

E-book: ISBN-13 978-1-64680-173-2

Cover image © Amber Knorr.

Cover and text design by Katherine Robinson.

Printed and bound in the United States of America.

Library of Congress Cataloging-in-Publication Data is available.

Contents

Foreword

"What are you looking for?"

These are the first words spoken by the Lord Jesus in the Gospel of John (Jn 1:38). He addressed them to the disciples of John the Baptist, who initially met the Lord on the road. Their response to Jesus's question was curious because they did not directly offer him an answer. Instead, they inquired as to where Jesus was staying, to which the Lord invited them with the simple words: "Come, and you will see" (Jn 1:39). Those who accept the Lord's invitation to come and see him will also receive the answer to his initial question. They will find what their hearts truly desire.

"What are you looking for?"

This is the question we must all face, despite our best efforts to dismiss it from our minds. Even the many distractions of modern life will not succeed in preventing us from confronting it. For it is a question of the heart that invites us to look deep within ourselves and to discover what really matters in life. It is the one and only question whose answer can change us forever.

In our modern world, many are tempted to answer this question by seeking the values of our secular, materialistic society. How many seek the comfort and security that comes from money, social acceptance, privilege, or an easy life, all while remaining unprepared to face the challenges and sufferings that inevitably come in life? How many times have you and I been distracted by the worries and problems of life and sought to answer this question in ways that gave us temporary relief and satisfaction but not true healing and peace?

For Padre Pio, the saintly friar whose life is narrated through the powerful stories found in this book, the answer to this question was a single word: Jesus. It was an answer that, for Padre Pio, never wavered and never changed despite the sufferings and challenges he endured. For Padre Pio, life was all about Jesus, who came to him as a small boy and whose presence permeated every aspect of the saint's life.

As you will read in this remarkable book, nothing else mattered to Padre Pio than to know, love, and serve the Lord. Through simplicity of life and his extraordinary miracles, St. Pio radiated a love for Jesus rooted in a simple, unwavering faith. One could say that Padre Pio found the foundation, purpose, and meaning of his life in the Christ Child, who was Love made flesh and born in the poverty of a manger. And when Padre Pio found the one whom his heart was truly looking for, he never looked for anything or anyone else.

"What are you looking for?"

The season of Advent is a time of prayer and reflection when we are invited to confront this one question as we journey to Bethlehem. We are encouraged to seek the answer that will truly satisfy the longings of our hearts and give us a peace that this world cannot give. For what we seek is not something but Someone, Christ the Lord, who is our Savior and Redeemer.

This book offers a remarkable invitation to journey during the days of Advent, accompanied by Padre Pio, to rediscover the simple answer to this question. It is an answer that transformed a young boy born in Pietrelcina into a saint. The same can happen to you and me if we are willing to seek, find, and stay with Jesus.

One of the great fallacies of modern life is the presumption that everything must be complicated. Perhaps this is true for the ways of the world. However, Padre Pio invites us on a simple journey to find what our hearts are looking for in Jesus. It is a journey that asks us to leave aside our presumptions, our distractions, and the values of our modern world. We are asked to walk with a simple faith that trusts that God loved us so much that he sent his only Son into the world so you and I might one day enjoy unending joy and peace. By walking this journey, you and I will eventually discover what Padre Pio found: the Lord himself walking with us every step of the way.

Through the insights offered in this book, Padre Pio is inviting us to begin a journey to find what our hearts are truly looking for. Are you and I willing to take the first step?

Most Reverend Frank J. Caggiano
Bishop of Bridgeport, Connecticut

INTRODUCTION

I'm not really sure when I first heard about Padre Pio. Most likely it was in my teenage years. At that time, Padre Pio was still alive, and stories came from Italy about him and the miracles associated with him. I was always curious about who he was, but being a teenager, I was preoccupied with my friends and other concerns, so I put any thoughts of Padre Pio aside.

In 1995, twenty-seven years after his death, I visited San Giovanni Rotondo for the first time. As I walked along the corridors of Padre Pio's convent, I could feel his presence everywhere. I heard stories about his mystical gifts and saw his clothing stained with blood from his stigmata. At first I wondered how it was possible for him to bear such pain, but then I saw the greatness of it all: he was able to bear the pain because he was never alone in his suffering. Our Lord and Our Lady were always at his side.

At times they were visibly present. Many times, during the course of Padre Pio's life, the Lord rewarded him by coming to him, often in the form of a little child. On many occasions, Padre Pio carried the child Jesus in his arms as he walked and prayed, his face glowing in ecstatic love for this child. His joy became indescribable when the Christ Child would appear to him on Christmas Eve. And so it should be for all of us—the anticipation of Advent, leading to the profound joy of receiving Jesus on Christmas Day.

Of course, Padre Pio's mystical gifts were both extraordinary and unique; most of us will never receive such a special visitation from the Christ Child during Advent. Instead, we set up our nativity scenes and wait with joyful anticipation for Christmas to arrive. I place many nativity scenes around my house during Advent; in these, I ceremoniously place the child Jesus in the manger at midnight on Christmas Eve. That loving gesture is a special moment for me, a moment when I can show my love for the child Jesus. This is a love that no one knew better than Padre Pio, who had the great fortune of holding this precious child in his arms on many occasions in his life.

Where did Padre Pio's great love of the Christ Child come from? To understand this, we need to go back to the beginning to the tiny hamlet of Pietrelcina, Italy, where we will find a child who would capture the minds and the hearts of people around the world. This child showed signs of extraordinary gifts of grace, and by the age of five, he dedicated his life to God. But who was this child, and why had he been chosen?

The Early Life of Padre Pio

On May 25, 1887, Francesco Forgione (Padre Pio) was born to Grazio and Maria Giuseppa Forgione. Francesco lived a simple Christian life. He was barely five years old when he began to cherish the idea of consecrating his life to God.

Francesco was a quiet child who loved to go to church and pray. As a young boy, he was able to see and communicate with not only his guardian angel but also Jesus and the Virgin Mary. He began to experience ecstasies and apparitions when he was just five years old, but for a long time, he did not tell anyone about them. When Padre Pio was asked why he hid these events that occurred at such an early age, he replied, "I thought such things happened to everyone."[1] It did not even occur to him that every child might not speak to Jesus and Mary in the same way that he did.

To little Francesco there was no greater holiday than Christmas, and he loved fashioning Nativity scenes. According to Fr. Joseph Mary Elder, "At his home in Pietrelcina, Francesco prepared the crib himself. He would often begin working on it as early as October. While pasturing the family's sheep with friends, he would search for clay to use to fashion the small statues of shepherds, sheep, and the magi. He took particular care in crafting the infant Jesus, making and remaking it continually until he felt he had it just right."[2] Why did Francesco model and remodel the clay? Perhaps because he knew the face of the Christ Child and wanted it to be a perfect image!

This simple faith of Padre Pio is at the heart of this book. The miracles associated with his ministry intrigue us, but it is the simplicity of his faith that keeps us coming back. How did such a humble man cause such a sensation in the world?

We need to move forward in Padre Pio's life to see how this happened and how Our Lord and Our Lady prepared him for the extraordinary life he would lead.

The Mystical Gifts of Padre Pio and the Stigmata

In September 1899 when Francesco received his first Holy Communion and Confirmation, something ripened in his innocent soul. Francesco was fifteen when he received an inward warning of the struggles he would have to endure with the devil: he would have to face Satan and choose a path to follow, a decision that was enlightened for him by the delicate touch of grace.

For Padre Pio, the celebration of Mass was the center of his spirituality. Padre Pio's Masses sometimes lasted for several hours. His Masses were truly the living Passion of Christ; during them, Padre Pio's stigmata would bleed. The parish priest in Pietrelcina called Padre Pio's Mass "an incomprehensible mystery."[3]

On September 20, 1918, while praying in the choir loft of the Church of Santa Maria delle Grazie, Padre Pio received the stigmata. Along with the stigmata came extraordinary spiritual gifts, including the gifts of healing, bilocation, and prophecy. When someone asked Padre Pio about these gifts, he replied, "You know, they are a mystery to me, too." Padre Pio never felt worthy of these gifts. He always remained humble.

One of the reasons Padre Pio's faith was so strong and his prayers were answered in such remarkable ways was that his whole life was one of prayer and wholehearted, simple service to Jesus and his mother. Padre Pio loved to pray the Rosary and recommended it to others. If someone asked what legacy he wished to leave to his spiritual children, he would reply, "My child, the Rosary."

By his example, Padre Pio showed all of us the way to make more room in our hearts for Jesus, whether during Advent and Christmas or at any time of year. He summed up the secret of his life with five simple words that became his greatest message to us: "Pray, hope, and don't worry!"

How Padre Pio Became a Saint

Early in the morning of September 23, 1968, Padre Pio made his last confession and renewed his Franciscan vows. As was customary, he had his rosary in his hands, though he did not have the strength to say the Hail Marys aloud. Till the end, he repeated the words *Gesù, Maria* ("Jesus, Mary"). Shortly before his death, he said, "I see two mothers," which was taken by those with him to mean his mother and Mary. At 2:30 a.m. he died in his cell in San Giovanni Rotondo. With his last breath he whispered, "Maria!"

Beginning in 1990, the Congregation for the Causes of Saints debated how Padre Pio had lived his life, and in

1997, Pope John Paul II declared him venerable. After examining the effects of his life as well as the reported healings associated with his intercession, John Paul II declared Padre Pio blessed in 1999. A final miracle, the healing of Matteo Pio Collela, led to John Paul II declaring Padre Pio a saint on June 16, 2002.

Along with Ray Ewen, who met Padre Pio during World War II, I attended the beatification and canonization ceremonies in Rome. At the canonization, the sea of people went from the doors of St. Peter's to the River Tiber—more than 300,000 people. How much people loved him! And how much he loved Jesus!

About This Book

In the next four weeks, we will listen to the words of Padre Pio. We will read about miracles, healings, and bilocations, as well as stories from people who knew Padre Pio and witnessed some of his miracles. Depending on the year, Advent can last between twenty-two and twenty-eight days, so this book contains reflections for twenty-eight days of Advent plus Christmas.

Each day of Advent, we will follow Padre Pio along the path that leads to Bethlehem. We experience the Lord's great love for Padre Pio in the many miracles that were granted in his name. We find a new Padre Pio in this book—not the Padre Pio who follows the Cross to Calvary but the Padre Pio who follows the Christ Child to

Bethlehem. No feast day was greater to Padre Pio than Christmas.

In the reflections, we experience the mystery of the birth of Our Lord. We experience not the great miracles that were granted through the intercession of Padre Pio but the great spiritual gifts Our Lord sends us each day. These spiritual blessings draw us closer to him on this journey to Bethlehem. We are also drawn closer to Christ through prayer. In this book, Padre Pio teaches us that we must continually pray. The miracles are a result of prayer.

My prayer for you is that this little book will help you keep your mind focused on Jesus, the Savior of the World, as you prepare to welcome him again into your home during this holy season of Advent and Christmas. Pray for the grace to be able to hold the Christ Child in your arms, as Padre Pio did, and to experience a heavenly peace.

Chronology

May 25, 1887	Francesco Forgione is born in Pietrelcina (Benevento), Italy, to Grazio Forgione and Maria Giuseppa (Peppa) Di Nunzio.
May 26, 1887	Francesco is baptized in the church of Sant'Anna.
January 6, 1903	Francesco enters the novitiate of the Capuchins in Morcone
January 22, 1903	Francesco takes the habit of the Capuchin order and the name of Brother Pio.
January 27, 1907	Brother Pio takes his final vows.
August 10, 1910	Brother Pio is ordained a priest in the cathedral of Benevento and is now known as Padre Pio.
August 14, 1910	Padre Pio says his first Mass in Pietrelcina.
September 8, 1911	Padre Pio, suffering from pains in his hands and feet, reveals to his spiritual adviser, Padre Benedetto from San Marco in Lamis, that he has had the

"invisible stigmata for about a year."

October 10, 1915	Padre Pio tells his superior that he has been suffering the pain inflicted by flagellations and the crowning of thorns for years.
February 17, 1916	Padre Pio is appointed to the monastery of Sant'Anna in Foggia.
July 28, 1916	During a period of suffocating heat, Padre Pio is taken to the monastery of San Giovanni Rotondo and stays there one week.
December 18, 1916	Padre Pio goes to Naples on national service, but his poor physical condition makes the doctors send him home on special leave.
November 12, 1917	Padre Pio returns to the monastery of San Giovanni Rotondo, where he stays until March 5, 1918, when he resumes national service in Naples.
March 16, 1918	Padre Pio returns to the monastery of San Giovanni Rotondo for good.

August 5, 1918	Padre Pio's heart is pierced by a spear by a mysterious celestial being, leaving him with a wound that bleeds for the rest of his life. This phenomenon is known as "transverberation."
September 20, 1918	Padre Pio's body is marked with stigmata, the visible signs of the Passion of Christ.
1919	News of Padre Pio's stigmata has spread throughout Italy, and thousands of pilgrims, attracted by this charismatic figure, begin to make their way to the Gargano.
May 15, 1919	The first examination of Padre Pio's stigmata is done by Professor Luigi Romanelli, a doctor and consultant at the hospital of Barletta.
July 26, 1919	Padre Pio is examined by Professor Amico Bignami, head of the medical pathology department of the University of Rome.
October 9, 1919	At the request of the general of the Capuchins, Padre Venanzio

	from Lisle-en-Rigault, Padre Pio undergoes in-depth medical examinations conducted by Dr. Giorgio Festa.
June 23, 1923	Padre Pio is debarred from saying Mass in public or replying to any of the letters arriving at the monastery in San Giovanni Rotondo.
June 25, 1923	A revolt breaks out in the afternoon when Padre Pio first says Mass in a private chapel rather than the church.
June 26, 1923	Padre Pio resumes saying Masses in the church.
August 8, 1923	Padre Pio is ordered to move to Ancona.
April 22, 1925	The faithful throughout Italy, resenting the restrictions placed on Padre Pio's confessional duties, are again in a state of turmoil.
July 16, 1933	Padre Pio resumes saying Mass in public following a two-year suspension.

January 9, 1940	Work is started on Padre Pio's "Casa Sollievo della Sofferenza" (House for the Relief of Suffering).
May 5, 1956	Casa Sollievo della Sofferenza is officially opened.
September 22, 1968	Padre Pio says his final Mass at 5:00 a.m.
September 23, 1968	Padre Pio dies at 2:30 a.m. His last words are "Jesus, Mary! Jesus, Mary!"
September 26, 1968	More than a hundred thousand people attend his funeral.
September 27, 1968	The crypt containing Padre Pio's body is opened to the public.
March 20, 1983	The official inquiry into Padre Pio's case is opened in San Giovanni Rotondo.
May 23, 1987	The Holy Father, John Paul II, makes a pilgrimage to San Giovanni Rotondo and prays at Padre Pio's tomb.
January 21, 1990	The beatification process is completed.
April 1997	Padre Pio is declared venerable.

May 2, 1999	Padre Pio of Pietrelcina is beatified by John Paul II.
June 16, 2002	Padre Pio of Pietrelcina is canonized by John Paul II and given the name St. Pio of Pietrelcina.
July 1, 2004	The new Sanctuary of St. Pio of Pietrelcina is consecrated in San Giovanni Rotondo.

Day 1

Every Day Is Advent

All of the feasts of the Church are beautiful . . . but Christmas has a tenderness, a childlike sweetness that captivates my entire heart!

—Padre Pio

In the heart of Padre Pio, every day was a kind of Advent. His simple, prayerful joy was rooted in the hope that he would one day be with Jesus and Mary in paradise. It was a hope that stayed with him no matter how much he suffered. And he suffered a great deal! People sometimes say that Padre Pio looked stern or angry in his photographs. Yet as those who knew him would often say, he never lost his childlike love for Jesus and his mother.

As we begin this journey through Advent with Padre Pio, let me introduce you to my dear friend Ray Ewen, who got to know the Capuchin friar and mystic while stationed near San Giovanni Rotundo during World War II. Seven times Ray served at Mass with Padre Pio in his chapel and witnessed Padre Pio's extraordinary spiritual gifts. Years later, I had the great pleasure of going with

Ray first to Padre Pio's beatification and later to the canonization in Rome.

Shortly after the canonization, Ray and I went to San Giovanni Rotondo to visit Padre Pio's home and the chapel in the old church of Santa Maria delle Grazie. The church and monastery date back to the sixteenth century. Near this chapel stands Padre Pio's private confessional. Numerous miracles took place in that confessional, where Padre Pio read the hearts of penitents and guided them to make a full confession. Many tears were shed, and most were tears of joy!

As we were leaving the chapel, I asked Ray what came to mind as he stood inside the chapel where he had so often seen Padre Pio serving on the altar. Ray looked at me and said, "The last time I saw him, before returning to the US, I remember thinking, *The next time I see him will be in paradise*." As he recalled this thought, Ray had tears in his eyes.

Many years would pass before Padre Pio's death in 1968. Yet Ray never forgot that moment of seeing that holy man on the altar and having the sense that he was in the presence of a man waiting to be called home. Years later, Ray was called home as well, holding fast to his hope of heaven just as Padre Pio did. I have no doubt Padre Pio was waiting for Ray when he arrived at the gates of paradise. May we all never lose sight of that great hope—the great hope that was born the day Love became incarnate in the womb of the Blessed Virgin Mary.

Read

In the sixth month, the angel Gabriel was sent from God to a town of Galilee called Nazareth, to a virgin betrothed to a man named Joseph, of the house of David, and the virgin's name was Mary. And coming to her, he said, "Hail, favored one! The Lord is with you." But she was greatly troubled at what was said and pondered what sort of greeting this might be.

—Luke 1:26–29

Reflect

May the Sweetest Child Jesus bring you all the graces, all the blessings, all the smiles that appeal to his infinite goodness.

—Padre Pio

During Advent, we return to the annunciation, the moment when Our Lady learns she is to be the mother of the Savior of the world. Take a few moments to ponder this great mystery, of the infant King who longs to live within your heart.

Advent is a time to reflect on the spiritual graces God sends to all of us—not the miraculous, extraordinary signs like healings and reading of hearts, such as those Padre Pio experienced, but the simple signs of the Spirit's presence in our lives. For which of those graces are you most thankful right now?

The gifts of Padre Pio were always used not to draw attention to himself but to draw his beloved sons and daughters closer to Jesus. How are you using your gifts to bless those around you?

Let Us Pray

Padre Pio, we pray you will stay close to us on this journey. We pray that we will arrive at Bethlehem with hearts full of hope, peace, joy, and love for the child Jesus!

Conclude your time of reflection and prayer with one Our Father, one Hail Mary, and one Glory Be.

DAY 2

Carry Jesus in Your Heart

Let us be very grateful to the Madonna because it is
she who gave us Jesus.

—Padre Pio

On numerous occasions I've walked along the corridors
of the convent of Santa Maria delle Grazie. The silence of
the corridors echoes the spirit of Padre Pio. I could sense
his presence in every step along the path that Padre Pio
would have followed to the choir loft and into the church
of Santa Maria delle Grazie. If you close your eyes, you
can imagine what it must have been like on those eve-
nings when Padre Pio walked these corridors. He was
on fire with the love of the Lord. And at Christmastime,
he glowed with the love of the child Jesus. The light that
encompassed his body held within it the precious Christ
Child. The child glowed with love for Padre Pio—a love
that Padre Pio knew from a very young age and that Jesus
shared with Padre Pio from his childhood.

Fr. Raffaele da Sant'Elia, who had the room next to
Padre Pio for thirty-five years at the convent, was an

eyewitness to a beautiful miracle in this corridor. He fondly recounts it for us:

> I had got up to go to the church for the Midnight Mass of 1924. The corridor was huge and dark, and the only illumination was the flame of a small oil lamp. Through the shadows I could see that Padre Pio, too, was making his way to the church. He had left his room and was making his way slowly along the corridor. I realized he was swathed in a band of light. I took a better look and saw that he had the baby Jesus in his arms. I just stood there, transfixed, in the doorway of my room and fell to my knees. Padre Pio passed by, all aglow. He didn't even notice I was there.[4]

Padre Pio's love for the child Jesus was almost childlike. The joy of Christmas stayed with him throughout the year and sustained him in his time of suffering. When we think of Padre Pio, we think of his stigmata and how he suffered for Jesus. But before the suffering, there was much joy. Through Our Lady, who never left his side, Padre Pio learned to love the child Jesus even as a very young child, when he was first able to communicate with Jesus and Mary. Padre Pio's love for Christmas grew out of the love he felt for Jesus—a great love that produced many spiritual and mystical fruits that blessed thousands of people, always bringing them closer to Jesus, just as Mary did.

Read

Then the angel said to her, "Do not be afraid, Mary, for you have found favor with God. Behold, you will conceive in your womb and bear a son, and you shall name him Jesus. He will be great and will be called Son of the Most High, and the Lord God will give him the throne of David his father, and he will rule over the house of Jacob forever, and of his kingdom there will be no end."

—Luke 1:30–33

Reflect

Far into the night, at the coldest time of the year, in a chilly grotto, more suitable for a flock of beasts than for humans, the promised Messiah—Jesus—the Savior of mankind, comes into the world in the fullness of time.
—Padre Pio

Today we reflect on the childlike innocence of Padre Pio. Never did it leave him. Just the thought of the child Jesus made him smile. To Padre Pio, each Christmas was a rebirth. A new beginning. Like Padre Pio, let our spirits be born again to a new life this Advent. Let us ask the Lord to come into our hearts and embrace us all with his heavenly blessings. And let us ask Our Lady to remain at our side as she remained at Padre Pio's side in very difficult moments.

Let us pray for our families, especially our children, on this journey to Bethlehem. May St. Joseph watch over our families and ask the Lord to protect them as he protected Our Lady on their journey to Bethlehem.

Let Us Pray

Padre Pio, we pray you will stay close to us on this journey. We pray that we will arrive at Bethlehem with hearts full of hope, peace, joy, and love for the child Jesus!

Conclude your time of reflection and prayer with one Our Father, one Hail Mary, and one Glory Be.

ᗞAY 3

ᒪook for the Christ Child

> May the child Jesus fill you with his divine charisma,
> make you experience the joys of the shepherds and the
> angels and fully bestow on you all the fire of that love
> which he made himself the least among us, and make
> you become a small child full of amiability, simplicity,
> love.
>
> —Padre Pio

Summers in San Giovanni Rotondo can be very humid.
Behind the old church of Santa Maria delle Grazie there
is a beautiful garden where Padre Pio would lunch when
the weather was warm. On pilgrimage, I and the pilgrims
who traveled with me always stopped in the garden to
meet with Fr. Ermelindo Di Capua, who blessed us with
Padre Pio's glove and shared with us beautiful memories
of Padre Pio.

Yesterday's reflection told the story of Padre Pio carrying the infant Jesus. Yet this was not an isolated inci-
dent. Many of Fr. Ermelindo's memories were of Padre
Pio embracing the child Jesus. There was nothing in life
Padre Pio loved more than the child Jesus. Padre Pio's

face would glow as he held the apparition in his arms! On
many occasions, people witnessed the child Jesus appear
in Padre Pio's arms. The Capuchins who lived with Padre
Pio had the great privilege of seeing many of these apparitions. Fr. Raffaele recorded one of these apparitions in
a manuscript:

> During the night of the 19th and 20th [September
> 1919] I could not sleep. I do not know why . . . perhaps
> it was because of the heat. Around midnight, I got up
> from my bed. I felt almost frightened. The hall was
> dark, broken only by the flickering light of a kerosene
> lamp. While I was in the doorway about to go out,
> Padre Pio passed by all radiant, with the child Jesus
> in his arms, walking slowly and praying. He passed in
> front of me, all radiant with light and he did not notice
> me. Only some years later, I came to know that, that
> 20th of September was the first anniversary of Padre
> Pio's stigmata.[5]

This miracle was not always clearly visible to those
nearby; Padre Pio would at times be seen with his arms
folded as though he were holding something. Many
Capuchins received special graces from God by witnessing Padre Pio walking in ecstasy, appearing to be holding
something invisible to the viewer in his arms. Can you
imagine witnessing this, knowing that the child Jesus is
in the arms of Padre Pio even though he is not visible?

We hold the child Jesus in our hearts and feel the
ecstasy of his presence every time we receive him in Holy

Communion. At this time if you close your eyes, he will become visible.

Read

But Mary said to the angel, "How can this be, since I have no relations with a man?" And the angel said to her in reply, "The holy Spirit will come upon you, and the power of the Most High will overshadow you. Therefore, the child to be born will be called holy, the Son of God."

—Luke 1:34–35

Reflect

There are none who clamour around him: only an ox and an ass lending their warmth to the newborn infant; with a humble woman, and a poor and tired man, in adoration beside him.

—Padre Pio

Today we reflect on Padre Pio's life as a child. As a young child, Padre Pio knew Jesus and Mary. What do you think little Francesco Forgione discussed with the child Jesus?

We sometimes hear stories of Jesus appearing as a child to the saints. Sr. Lucia, visionary of Fatima, recounted how the child Jesus would appear to her. She said they would play together in the garden at her convent in Pontevedra. (Sr. Lucia was barely a teenager when she entered the convent.) Was Jesus a playmate for Francesco too?

Think about the little clay figures that little Francesco made for his Nativity. He would continually reshape the clay figure of Jesus until it was right. He was sure he knew what the child Jesus looked like! How amazing is that?

Today, let us think about how we would greet the child Jesus. Let us reshape in our minds the image of the child Jesus until it is a perfect image, and let us follow that perfect image to Bethlehem.

Let Us Pray

Padre Pio, we pray you will stay close to us on this journey. We pray that we will arrive at Bethlehem with hearts full of hope, peace, joy, and love for the child Jesus!

Conclude your time of reflection and prayer with one Our Father, one Hail Mary, and one Glory Be.

Day 4

Fix Your Eyes on the Manger!

As the days pass, I see ever more clearly the greatness of God, and in this light, which grows brighter and brighter, my soul burns with the desire to be united to him by indissoluble bonds.

—Padre Pio

In 1919 a priest named Padre Carlo Naldi brought his friend, a Jewish man named Lello Pegna, to visit Padre Pio. The priest told Padre Pio that Pegna had recently become totally blind. The priest had brought him to Padre Pio in the hopes of his friend being cured.

Padre Pio told Pegna, "The Lord will not grant you the grace of physical sight unless you first receive sight for your soul. After you are baptized, then the Lord will give you your sight."

A few months later, Pegna returned. He did not have the dark glasses that he normally wore because of his blindness. Pegna explained to Padre Pio that, despite opposition from his family, he had become a Christian and was baptized. Immediately after his baptism, he was discouraged when his blindness continued, but after a

13

number of months, his sight returned. The physician who had earlier told Pegna that he was hopelessly blind now had to admit that his eyesight was in perfect condition.

A priest named Fr. Paolino kept in contact with Lello Pegna for nearly thirty years, and reported that his vision remained perfect for the rest of his life.

Read

The Mighty One has done great things for me, and holy is his name. His mercy is from age to age to those who fear him. He has shown might with his arm, dispersed the arrogant of mind and heart.

—Luke 1:49–51

Reflect

Nothing can be heard except the sobs and whimpers of the infant God. And by means of his crying and weeping he offers to the Divine justice the first ransom for our redemption.

—Padre Pio

Today, let us reflect on Padre Pio's words: "First receive sight for your soul."

Can we imagine how it was for Lello Pegna to hear these words? We know he came to believe. We know he sought sight for his soul, but did he immediately believe? Did he understand Padre Pio's words, and did he believe that if he accepted the Lord, he would be cured?

Did Pegna agree to be baptized just to regain his sight? I don't think that at all. Why? We know Padre Pio could read hearts. I believe Padre Pio knew that this man's faith was always there, and he only needed to reach into his soul to find what he was missing: not just his eyesight but also the sight of the Lord, who could see into the man's soul and who was always there, waiting to be found.

The Lord sees all that is in our souls, but do we see the presence of the Lord there? When we are in doubt and we are searching for the Lord, we need go no further than our souls, where the Lord dwells and joins himself to us. The Lord puts before us many wondrous things, but sometimes we miss them because we forget to search within ourselves for his presence. We need to open our hearts and our souls to the Lord so we can see all that he has prepared for us in life. Lello Pegna always had the Lord in his soul, but he didn't know the Lord was there. Yet he believed in the words of Padre Pio, and he opened his soul to the Lord who was waiting there for him. Once his soul was opened, he was able to see and feel the presence of the Lord within him.

Do you see the presence of the Lord within you? Have you properly prepared a place in your soul for your redeemer? Before Our Lord enters into your soul, he must be invited. At the altar, when you receive Our Lord, do you invite him to a special place in your soul?

On this journey to Bethlehem, let us open our minds and souls to Jesus. On Christmas Day, let us invite Jesus to our Feast of Love where he, the Christ Child, reigns.

Let Us Pray

Padre Pio, we pray you will stay close to us on this journey. We pray that we will arrive at Bethlehem with hearts full of hope, peace, joy, and love for the child Jesus!

Conclude your time of reflection and prayer with one Our Father, one Hail Mary, and one Glory Be.

DAY 5

A Grieving Mother's Hope

> Keep your eyes fixed on him who is your guide to the heavenly country, where he is leading you. What does it matter to you whether Jesus wishes to guide you to Heaven by way of the desert or by the meadow, so long as he is always with you and you arrive at the possession of a blessed eternity?
>
> —Padre Pio

We find peace in our faith, even when the road is very hard and painful to walk. This is a story told by Camille Loccisano, who lost her son to cancer when he was only seventeen years old. She writes:

My son Frankie was diagnosed with osteosarcoma (bone cancer) in July of 2005. He fought a long and hard battle against this illness for twenty-seven months. He had four lung surgeries, his leg amputated, radiation, and countless rounds of chemotherapy. He also developed a secondary cancer, leukemia. During his ordeal, Frankie kept hopeful and prayerful. He kept Jesus as the center of his life and prayed to his patron saint, Padre Pio, whose picture he always kept with him. Frankie died on September 14, 2007. The morning of Frankie's Mass of Christian Burial, my family and I were at the funeral home where there had been a public viewing of Frankie for two days. When it was almost time to say goodbye to my son and go to St. Ephrem's in Brooklyn for the funeral Mass, I felt my strength failing me. I dreaded this final time, knowing I would never see my son again. At that moment I prayed to Padre Pio, begging him to help me.

The moment I finished my prayer, into the funeral home walked Ray Ewen. Ray had met Padre Pio in 1945 when he served in the US military in Italy. Ray prayed for my son, and he prayed for me. As he prayed, I felt a great sense of peace come over me, and I received the strength I needed so badly.

Ray does not live close by, but he told me that when he woke up that morning, he felt a very strange urge to get to the funeral home and see Frankie. It was not easy for him, but he managed to find a ride with a close friend who was also very devoted to Padre Pio.

It wasn't long afterward that I had a vivid dream about my son. In it, Frankie looked well and breathed easily. I thought he was alive again. He let me know that he was in heaven and only back to speak to me for a moment. He told me he was in a place so beautiful that it was impossible to describe. He also told me he was with other children. I asked him if Padre Pio was there. Frankie looked at me and said, "Padre Pio was there to meet me when I arrived."

Read

Peace I leave with you; my peace I give to you. Not as the world gives do I give to you. Do not let your hearts be troubled or afraid.

—John 14:27

Reflect

There is something very peaceful about this story Camille shared. When we read the story, we might think of Calvary for all the suffering Frankie went through, but in fact, this is a joyful story. Think of the faith of this young man. Think about his mother's dream of him in heaven. From sorrow there came joy!

On this journey to Bethlehem, let us find peace even when we hit a bump in the road or it seems as if our journey has been completely rerouted. No journey is perfect, but it can be if we open up our hearts to Jesus. Let us call on Our Lady to join us and bring peace to our hearts from her son, Jesus. At the end of this journey, the child Jesus is waiting for you. Find the peaceful path and follow it. You will be amazed at what awaits you along the road.

Let Us Pray

Padre Pio, we pray you will stay close to us on this journey. We pray that we will arrive at Bethlehem with hearts full of hope, peace, joy, and love for the child Jesus!

Conclude your time of reflection and prayer with one Our Father, one Hail Mary, and one Glory Be.

DAY 6

Hope from a War-Torn Land

Don't worry about anything.

—Padre Pio

Zina Hallak has experienced through her mother the peace that Padre Pio offers from God. She tells us:

I was born near Baghdad, Iraq, and baptized in the parish of the Virgin Mary of the Holy Heart. When I was still a baby, my parents decided to move the family to the United States to escape the dangers of the country and so my brothers and sisters and I might have a better life. It was a great sacrifice for them to leave their country and all that was dear to them, but they knew it was for the best.

I learned about Padre Pio in 2006 and started attending the Padre Pio prayer group in San Diego, California. On occasion, I brought my mother with me, and she liked it very much. The following year, 2007, was a devastating year for the Chaldean Catholic community in Baghdad. My mother became very distraught over the tragedies occurring there. Chaldean Catholic bishops, priests, and deacons were threatened daily. Extremist terrorist groups warned them that they would be killed if they continued to have Mass in their churches.

My mother watched the news on television one day and saw several of the Catholic churches in Baghdad that were destroyed by roadside bombings. She was filled with anxiety and wept over the tragic events. She had a great love for the parish she had attended when she lived in Iraq and feared that it would also be leveled just like the others. One evening when my mother was very sad, I took her to the Padre Pio prayer group with me. When we came home, I placed a picture of Padre Pio next to my parents' bed.

That night she had a vivid dream. In her dream, she was praying, pleading that God would protect her parish in Baghdad. Padre Pio suddenly appeared in her dream. He raised his hands, and she could see the marks of the stigmata. He said to her in Aramaic, "Do not worry. There will be victory." When my mother woke up, she was filled with a great sense of peace.

My parents' parish in Baghdad is still standing today. Although one window was shattered and an outer wall was damaged by an act of violence, the church was repaired and Mass is said there regularly. My parents have remained very devoted to Padre Pio.

Read

And let the peace of Christ control your hearts, the peace into which you were also called in one body. And be thankful.

—Colossians 3:15

Reflect

Today, let us reflect on our freedom to worship as we wish, and let us pray this freedom will never be taken from us.

In the United States, we take everything for granted. Over the course of the COVID-19 pandemic, we have experienced church closings not for terror but for pandemic, and this threw us into a panic. What will happen? When will we return to our places of worship? Think of what you missed most in this time. We were able to watch the Mass on TV and on our computers, but we were deprived of Our Lord. We were deprived of the Eucharist. We found it very difficult. While churches in America have opened again, we need to think about people like Zina's family who are in constant fear of their churches closing. They fear for their lives every time they walk into a church. They fear that their Christmas Masses will be interrupted by terrorists who will arrest their priests and close their churches.

On this Advent journey, let us keep in mind the Church in the Middle East. The persecuted Church. In the Old Testament, our ancestors in faith came from the regions along the Tigris and Euphrates rivers. These people were Our Lord's people, and we need to keep them in our prayers.

Let us pray to the child Jesus that the people who live where Our Lord did will find peace in this Christmas season.

Let Us Pray

Padre Pio, we pray you will stay close to us on this journey. We pray that we will arrive at Bethlehem with hearts full of hope, peace, joy, and love for the child Jesus!

Conclude your time of reflection and prayer with one Our Father, one Hail Mary, and one Glory Be.

DAY 7

Running on Empty

Faith is the light which shines at the highest peak of
every soul acceptable to our Father.

—Padre Pio

Fr. Onorato had been to San Giovanni Rotondo on other
occasions, but this time it would be different. On this visit
with Padre Pio, Fr. Onorato tells us a miracle happened,
and in this miracle, we can see the humor of Padre Pio.
Let's listen to Fr. Onorato relate his story:

> I went to San Giovanni Rotondo with a friend of mine
> by motorcycle. We arrived at the convent some min-
> utes before noon. After paying my respects to the supe-
> rior, I went to the refectory to meet Padre Pio in order
> to kiss his hand. It should be taken into account that
> my model motorbike was called a "wasp." Padre Pio
> told me: "Son, did the 'wasp' sting you?" I was quite
> surprised because Padre Pio had not seen me when
> I arrived at the convent, but he knew what kind of
> transportation I had used to get there.
>
> The next morning, we left San Giovanni Rotondo
> on my "wasp" motorbike and set out for San Michel,

a little town not far from San Giovanni Rotondo. The gasoline tank was going empty, so we decided to fill up at Monte Saint Angelo. But as soon as we reached that little town, we had a bad surprise: all the gas stations were closed. At that point we decided to go back to San Giovanni Rotondo and hoped to find somebody along the road who could provide us with some gasoline. I was worried about my brothers in the convent; it would be ungracious not to be back at the convent by lunchtime, for they were waiting for me. But low on gas, the engine started to make noise, and after a few feet it stopped altogether. We checked the tank; it was empty. With sadness I pointed out to my friend that we had only fifteen minutes to reach the convent and take part in the lunch with our brothers. We could not find any solution, and for this reason my friend stomped on the starter pedal. Unbelievable! The motorbike started again! We immediately set out for San Giovanni Rotondo without asking ourselves how the motorbike had started without gasoline.

When we arrived in the middle of the square of the convent, the motorbike stopped working again. We opened the tank and realized it was still as dry as it was before. We were also astonished when we looked at our watches: it was ten minutes before lunchtime. That meant we had covered fifteen kilometers in five minutes: an average of 180 kilometers per hour. Without gasoline! I entered the convent as the brothers were coming down for lunch; and when I went to meet Padre Pio, he was watching me and smiling.

Read

Then the peace of God that surpasses all understanding will guard your hearts and minds in Christ Jesus.

—Philippians 4:7

Reflect

I feel a great desire to abandon myself with greater trust to the Divine Mercy and to place my hope in God alone.

—Padre Pio

Padre Pio certainly had a great sense of humor. The amazing thing about this story is Fr. Onorato and his friend never asked the Lord for help, but the engine started. Was Padre Pio with them on the journey? We know he could read hearts. Could he also read minds and so know they were in trouble?

Let's think about how we pray. Many times, we don't ask the Lord for the things we need even though our hearts are heavy. Somehow the Lord just knows our needs.

On this Advent journey, let us ask the Lord to read the hearts and mind of those who will travel with us to Bethlehem. Let's pray that the child Jesus will stay with us and watch out for us along the way. May the manger be the focus of our journey and the child Jesus our reward.

Let Us Pray

Padre Pio, we pray you will stay close to us on this journey. We pray that we will arrive at Bethlehem with hearts full of hope, peace, joy, and love for the child Jesus!

Conclude your time of reflection and prayer with one Our Father, one Hail Mary, and one Glory Be.

Day 8

She Will Draw Water from the Well

Jesus will assist you and give you the grace to live a heavenly life and nothing whatever will be able to separate you from His love.

—Padre Pio

Rosa del Popolo relates the story of her cousin Sara, who was concerned she wouldn't be able to become a nun and found encouragement in the words of Padre Pio:

Padre Pio is no stranger to my family. In the 1950s, my cousin Sara wanted desperately to become a nun but could not leave home because of her mother's very poor health. Sara was taking care of her, and she did not feel she could leave her to enter the convent. She wanted to talk to Padre Pio about it, so she and her father traveled by train from their home in Sant'Alfio, Sicily, to speak to him. During the train ride, Sara and her father had something to eat, and her father accidently spilled some wine on his clothing. Sara felt very embarrassed at the thought that Padre Pio might see the wine stains on her father's clothing or, even worse, that they would greet Padre Pio with her father smelling of wine. She gave her father a scolding.

When they were finally able to speak to Padre Pio, he assured her that she would be able to enter the convent and that Rosa, her mother, would be fine. In fact, Padre Pio told them that upon their return home, they would find Rosa drawing water from the well. This was impossible for her to do since she suffered from serious heart problems and was too weak to perform even the simplest and most menial tasks.

During their conversation, Padre Pio told Sara not to ever again scold her father. My cousin was shocked that Padre Pio knew this had happened on the train.

When they returned home, they found Rosa drawing water from the well just as Padre Pio assured them. Rosa regained her health immediately and miraculously. Sara was able to leave home and enter the convent.

Rosa also has said that she is proud to have experienced Padre Pio's love and intercession in her own life and in the lives of her immediate family. They too have received many graces through the intercession of Padre Pio.

Read

If you knew the gift of God and who is saying to you, "Give me a drink," you would have asked him and he would have given you living water.

—John 4:10

Reflect

Sara hoped she would be able to become a nun, but she feared it would not be possible because of her mother's poor health. Padre Pio gave Sara hope. Rosa "will draw water from the well"!

This leads us to the story of the woman at the well, which is one of the most iconic encounters with Jesus in the Bible. It is also the longest encounter between Jesus and any other person in the Gospel of John. It is an important encounter because of what it reveals.

Jesus told the Samaritan woman not only that he was the Son of God and the Messiah but also that he had come to offer living water, the kind that "will become in [them] a spring of water welling up to eternal life" (Jn 4:14). Why did Jesus say this to the Samaritan woman? Jesus could see the ache in her heart. He knew she was unhappy in her life but that she could see no other way of living. Through the "living water" she would find a new life, one that pleases the Lord.

Similarly, Padre Pio saw the ache in Sara's heart and reassured her that the "Living Water" she wished to be near also desired to have her near him.

As we continue on this Advent journey, let us open our hearts and invite the "Living Water" to be near us and well up in us hope for eternal life.

Let Us Pray

Padre Pio, we pray you will stay close to us on this journey. We pray that we will arrive at Bethlehem with hearts full of hope, peace, joy, and love for the child Jesus!

Conclude your time of reflection and prayer with one Our Father, one Hail Mary, and one Glory Be.

DAY 9

The Three Miracles

My past, O Lord, to your mercy; my present to your
love; my future to your providence.

—Padre Pio

Bari, Italy, during the Second World War, housed the
headquarters of the American Air Force General Command. Bari is about 150 kilometers south of San Giovanni
Rotondo, and many officers were said to have been saved
by Padre Pio during the war. Even the general commander
had been a witness to one amazing episode.

The American commanding officer wanted to lead
a squadron of bombardiers to destroy a depot of German war material that had been located in San Giovanni
Rotondo. The general said, "When the airplanes were near
the target, he and his men saw in the sky a monk with
uplifted hands. The bombs dropped away by themselves
and fell into the woods. The airplanes reversed course
without being maneuvered by the pilots or by the other
officers." All wondered who that monk was whom the
airplanes had obeyed. Someone told the general, "At San
Giovanni Rotondo there is a monk who works miracles,"

and he decided that, as soon as the country had been freed, he would have to go to see if he was the same monk they had seen in the sky.

After the war, the general went to the Capuchin monastery with some pilots. Just entering the sacristy, the general found himself in front of various monks, one of whom he immediately recognized as the monk who had stopped his airplanes: Padre Pio walked toward him and, as he approached the general, asked, "Are you the one who wanted to kill all of us?" Relieved by the padre's lighthearted remark and kind expression, the general knelt in front of him. As usual Padre Pio spoke to him in Italian, but the general was convinced the monk had spoken in English. This was another one of Padre Pio's gifts. The two became friends, and the general, who was Protestant, became Catholic.

Read

This is the day the Lord has made; let us rejoice in it and be glad.

—Psalm 118:24

Reflect

It is now God himself who acts and operates directly in the depths of my soul, without the ministry of the senses, either interior or exterior. . . . All I can say of this present state is that my soul has no concern for anything but God.

—Padre Pio

Notice how the general recounts the story in such a calm manner. It seems impossible to me that these pilots would have just taken the whole situation in stride. I would think they went back to the base delirious.

Could you imagine their shock? Bombs were dropping on their own. The planes reversed and went back to the base. Yet through it all, the general doesn't seem alarmed. Yes, he did say he would investigate, but no, he didn't seem shaken. Instead of dropping everything for an answer, he waits until the war is over, and he goes to find the mysterious monk.

There are three miracles in this story. The first is the events in the sky that saved the people of San Giovanni Rotondo. The second is that Padre Pio is speaking in Italian and the general understands every word, as he said, in English. The third is the miracle of conversion.

The Lord certainly works in strange ways. This was obviously a soul he wanted. But I also believe it was a soul looking for a home because, when the general saw Padre Pio, he immediately knelt before him for his blessing. He immediately opened his heart to the Lord. Rather than feeling fear at Padre Pio's words, the general felt relief that he had found the right man.

On our Advent journey, let us seek out those who are waiting for a home for their souls. Let us never waste an opportunity to speak about the Lord and open the hearts and minds of those around us. In your search for the child Jesus, keep your heart open to those who are wandering the path in search of Our Lord.

Let Us Pray

Padre Pio, we pray you will stay close to us on this journey. We pray that we will arrive at Bethlehem with hearts full of hope, peace, joy, and love for the child Jesus!

Conclude your time of reflection and prayer with one Our Father, one Hail Mary, and one Glory Be.

DAY 10

A Grandmother's Faith

> As the days pass, I see ever more clearly the greatness
> of God, and in this light, which grows brighter and
> brighter, my soul burns with the desire to be united
> to him by indissoluble bonds.
>
> —Padre Pio

We talk in the Church about the faith of parents and how,
through their prayers, their children are cured. But let's
not forget about the faith of our grandparents, as many
children have been saved by their grandparent's prayers.

Gemma di Giorgi was born without pupils in her eyes,
a condition declared to be incurable by a number of specialists and that left her unable to see. Yet in this miracle,
we meet a child who was able to see.

At the age of seven, Gemma's grandmother brought
her to meet Padre Pio. About halfway there, for the first
time in her life, Gemma began to see. Gemma's grandmother and other friends marveled at this miraculous
occurrence; they called it a miracle! When Gemma
arrived, Padre Pio, although he had never seen her before,
called Gemma by name in front of the congregation at

church and heard her confession. During the confession, even though Gemma mentioned nothing of her blindness, Padre Pio made the Sign of the Cross over each eye. At the end of the confession, he blessed her and said, "Be good and saintly."

Decades after this event, Gemma still sees perfectly, despite her continued lack of pupils, and undergoes eye examinations by specialists who agree there is no explanation for her ability to see. Gemma's grandmother has said, "Many eye doctors have arrived here in our home, and all have declared the same thing: that without pupils in one's eyes one should not be able to see and that, therefore, this is a miracle."

Read

I will praise you, Lord, with all my heart; I will declare all your wondrous deeds.

—Psalm 9:2

Reflect

When I was a child, I went to visit my grandparents on a Sunday. That's how it was with most families: Sunday was spent at grandma's house. In this day and age, it's different. Many grandparents play a very important role in the lives of their grandchildren. With both parents working, it is not always possible to use day care or, in many cases, parents don't want to use it. So we find more and more grandparents taking on the role of care provider. It could be as simple as taking the children to school and picking them up or, in other cases, the grandparent may be living with the family.

I was a CCD teacher for more than twenty-five years. In that time, I came to realize that many children came to the sacraments because of their grandparents. Their grandparents brought them to religious instructions: some out of necessity because the children's parents worked and others because they knew that if they didn't bring them, their grandchildren would not receive the sacraments. And so, it is because of these grandparents that the children attended CCD and received the sacraments.

Today let us reflect on and be grateful for the faith of our grandparents!

In our story today we see a grandmother bringing her grandchild to Padre Pio in the hope he will pray for a cure for her. What's so interesting about the story is her granddaughter is already cured before she arrives. Faith is the key. Gemma's grandmother had faith that her grandchild could see against all odds. Remember, this child had no pupils, and it is not possible to see without pupils. Yet, as scripture tells us numerous times, "nothing will be impossible for God" (see Lk 1:37).

As we are on our Advent journey today, let us pray for all grandparents who make sacrifices to bring their grandchildren to the faith. Let us pray on this road to

Bethlehem that our children and all those who have lost their faith will find it again in this Christmas season.

Let Us Pray

Padre Pio, we pray you will stay close to us on this journey. We pray that we will arrive at Bethlehem with hearts full of hope, peace, joy, and love for the child Jesus!

Conclude your time of reflection and prayer with one Our Father, one Hail Mary, and one Glory Be.

Day 11

Messages of the Angels

> Invoke your Guardian Angel who will enlighten you.
> God gave you your Guardian Angel for this reason. So,
> make use of your Angel's services.
>
> —Padre Pio

For many years Padre Alessio Parente ran the English office at San Giovanni Rotondo. I had the pleasure of meeting with Padre Alessio on many occasions, and it was clear in our interactions that his one goal in life was to see Padre Pio's glorification.

Padre Alessio was Padre Pio's indispensable assistant for the last six years of his life. Padre Pio told one of his spiritual children that Padre Alessio took care of him with great solicitude, like a "faithful puppy." Padre Alessio was filled with joy when he learned Padre Pio had said this about him and treasured the words for the rest of his life.

After visiting Padre Pio's tomb, other pilgrims and I would immediately go to the English office to meet with Padre Alessio and listen to his stories about Padre Pio. His hospitality, patience, and complete commitment to his work created happy memories for all of us. There were many English-speaking pilgrims, all of whom sought his attention to listen to their story or to share their problems. In him we saw a glimpse of the demands made on his beloved mentor, Padre Pio.

Padre Pio was Padre Alessio's mission in life. Promoting Padre Pio's teachings and lessons, which of course was the Gospel of Jesus, was his very reason for living. On one occasion, Padre Alessio related this story to us:

> I was sitting by Padre Pio's side on the verandah near his room. . . . I saw Padre Pio was fingering his rosary, and there was such peace and calm around him that I felt encouraged to approach him and ask some questions. At this time, I would receive many letters asking me to seek Padre Pio's advice on a problem of some sort.
>
> On this occasion when I approached him, he replied, "Come on, my son, leave me alone. Don't you see I am very busy?" *Strange*, I thought. He was sitting down fingering his rosary and he says he is busy. I remained silent thinking, *It is not true that he is busy*. Padre Pio turned to me and said, "Didn't you see all the guardian angels going backward and forward from my spiritual children bringing messages from them?" Surprised by his words, I retorted, "Father, I have not seen even one guardian angel, but I believe you because you tell people every day to send you theirs."

Read

For the kingdom of God is not a matter of food and drink, but of righteousness, peace, and joy in the holy Spirit.

—Romans 14:17

Reflect

Jesus, our dear Mother, my little angel, St. Joseph, and our father, St. Francis, are almost always with me.

—Padre Pio

Today let us reflect on the presence of our guardian angels.

Padre Pio wrote in a letter to Raffaelina Cerase, "How close to us stands one of the celestial spirits, who from the cradle to the grave never leaves us for an instant. He guides us, he protects us like a friend, like a brother. This should be a source of constant consolation for us, especially during the saddest times of our lives."[6]

Padre Pio said that he was grateful for his own guardian angel's presence in every situation, no matter how difficult the circumstances. During his childhood, he recalled, he had gotten to know his guardian angel through prayer and meditation and developed a close bond with his guardian angel. "My guardian angel has been my friend since my infancy," he said.

Guardian angels assure us of the presence of God. So let us go forward on this journey in the presence of our guardian angel. May our guardian angels lead us to Bethlehem, where we will meet the choir of angels who will deliver us to the child Jesus.

Let Us Pray

Padre Pio, we pray you will stay close to us on this journey. We pray that we will arrive at Bethlehem with hearts full of hope, peace, joy, and love for the child Jesus!

Conclude your time of reflection and prayer with one Our Father, one Hail Mary, and one Glory Be.

$\big)$AY 12

$\wedge$ Healing Gift of the Heart

Walk the way of the Lord in simplicity, do not torment
your spirit.

—Padre Pio

Padre Pio sought the help of his close friends and collab-
orators and worked for many years in order to achieve his
dream of establishing a fully equipped, modern hospital
in San Giovanni Rotondo. When it was built, he named
it the Home for the Relief of Suffering. On the day of its
inauguration, May 5, 1956, Padre Pio offered Mass on the
front steps of the hospital while a crowd of fifteen thousand people looked on. Many people wanted to help Padre
Pio in his great work, as evidenced by the following story:

Donato Di Ge visited San Giovanni Rotondo on January 20, 1960. It was a Sunday, and he was spurred on
by the usual irresistible desire to be near Padre Pio. In
the sacristy of the church, he noticed posters everywhere asking for blood donors for the Casa Sollievo
della Sofferenza—the Home for the Relief of Suffering. Donato wanted with all his heart to answer the
call of the hospital; however, he had recently had an

operation for a perforated ulcer and had nearly died. He also had other health problems, including very low blood pressure and chronic pain in his gallbladder. He decided it would be best to consult Padre Pio about the matter. Shortly after Mass, Donato was able to speak to Padre Pio. Donato told Padre Pio about his various health issues and then asked him if it would be all right for him to be a blood donor for the hospital. Padre Pio looked at him with a penetrating gaze and then said to him kindly, "Well, what are you waiting for?"

Donato went straight over to the hospital where the doctor in charge gave him a physical examination. When the doctor took his blood pressure and saw how low it was, he explained the hospital's policy to Donato. "I am very sorry," the doctor said. "Because you have an abnormal blood pressure reading, you will not be allowed to be a donor." "Doctor," Donato replied, "I spoke to Padre Pio about this a few moments ago, and he wanted me to come over here to see you."

The doctor had great faith in Padre Pio. If Padre Pio had encouraged Donato to donate his blood, it was good enough for the doctor. He told Donato that he would give his approval. As Donato continued to donate blood to Padre Pio's hospital, his blood pressure showed a marked improvement and the chronic pain that had plagued him for such a long time began to diminish. In other words, the more blood he gave, the better his health became. He was able to make fifty-two blood donations to the hospital.

Read

For nothing will be impossible for God.

—Luke 1:37

Reflect

Let us be especially grateful to God for the gift of faith,
a gift which is mainly instilled in us with Baptism.

—Padre Pio

This is just one of many stories where people put their faith in Padre Pio, even though others told them they should not do what he guided them to do. In this case, the doctor who told Donato he could not give blood because of abnormal blood pressure, in fact, changed his mind when he heard that Padre Pio said Donato should give blood. The doctor had great faith in Padre Pio. The doctor trusted the word of Padre Pio and took Donato's blood.

Faith! Our faith allows us to trust even in situations where there is doubt! Through faith we find joy! Look at what happened to Donato. The more blood Donato donated, the more his blood pressure improved and the chronic pain that had plagued him diminished.

On this Advent journey, let our faith guide us and let us follow Padre Pio to the stable at Bethlehem.

Let Us Pray

Padre Pio, we pray you will stay close to us on this journey. We pray that we will arrive at Bethlehem with hearts full of hope, peace, joy, and love for the child Jesus!

Conclude your time of reflection and prayer with one Our Father, one Hail Mary, and one Glory Be.

Day 13

Open Our Eyes to See

Lord God of my heart, you alone know and see all my troubles. You alone are aware that all my distress springs from my fear of losing you, of offending you, from my fear of not loving you as much as I should love and desire to love you. If you, to whom everything is present and who alone can see the future, know that it is for your greater glory and for my salvation that I should remain in this state, then let it be so. I don't want to escape from it.

—Padre Pio

Grazia was a peasant who was twenty-nine years old. She had been blind from birth. She used to go to the little church of the convent in order to meet Padre Pio.

Once Padre Pio asked her if she wanted to see. "Of course I would!" answered the woman, "but I want to see only if this is not due to me, not to any pity." "Well, you will recover," said Padre Pio, and he sent her to Bari, Italy, where there was a very good doctor who was the husband of one of Padre Pio's friends. But the doctor, after checking the patient's eyes, told his wife, "There's no hope for this girl! Padre Pio can heal her only by a miracle, but I must send her back home without operating on her."

His wife insisted he try to help Grazia, saying, "But if Padre Pio has sent her to you, you could at least try to operate on her, at least on one of her eyes." The doctor agreed and operated on both of her eyes. The operations were successful, and Grazia's eyes were healed! For the first time in her life, she could see. When she was back in San Giovanni Rotondo, she ran to the convent and knelt down at Padre Pio's feet. He ordered her to stand up. She told him, "Bless me, Father. Bless me!" So he marked the Sign of the Cross on her, but she still waited to be blessed. When she was blind, Padre Pio used to bless her by making the Sign of the Cross on her head with his hand, and she wanted him to bless her in that same way. When he realized what she was waiting for, Padre Pio asked, "How do you want to be blessed? With a bucket of water poured on your head?"

Read

Although you have not seen him you love him; even though you do not see him now yet believe in him, you rejoice with an indescribable and glorious joy, as you attain the goal of [your] faith, the salvation of your souls.

—1 Peter 1:8–9

Reflect

May the Lord confirm with His blessings, these wishes
of mine, for your happiness is very close to my heart
and I work and pray continuously for this end.

—Padre Pio

Let us reflect on this amazing miracle today!

Grazia was blind from birth. She knew that Padre Pio
was able to ask the Lord to heal her, yet she never asked
for a healing. Here's what makes this miracle interesting:
Grazia was happy to live with her blindness as long as the
Lord wanted. She almost saw it as a gift, and she feared
that the blindness would be taken away for the wrong
reason, such as out of pity! Her faith cured her.

Let us hope we can find such faith—so we can trust
that even when things are not good or not going our way,
the Lord has a reason for what he is giving us, and we will
see his purpose along the way. Let us also have faith to
trust when the Lord is guiding us to change.

On this Advent journey to Bethlehem, let us find joy
in remembering the great faith of Grazia. Let us also put
all our trust and faith in the Lord that he will always show
us the path that is best for us, even when it is not the path
we would choose.

Let Us Pray

Padre Pio, we pray you will stay close to us on this journey. We pray that we will arrive at Bethlehem with hearts full of hope, peace, joy, and love for the child Jesus!

Conclude your time of reflection and prayer with one Our Father, one Hail Mary, and one Glory Be.

DAY 14

Stay with Me Lord

Stay with me, Lord, because I am weak and I need your strength, that I may not fall so often.

—Padre Pio

Deacon Ron Allen worked as a volunteer chaplain at a local hospital. One time, when he went to the hospital, there was a note for him that one of the patients requested a visit. The deacon recalled:

I went to the room and found a very nice-looking young man in his late twenties who was in the hospital for drug-related problems. He told me he was in a lot of pain and was very depressed because he had a relapse and had started using drugs again. He was so happy I had come to visit him. He told me his father had introduced him to hard drugs when he was just thirteen years old, and they used drugs together on a regular basis. He said he went into cardiac arrest four times and at one point had been declared clinically dead. He had a stroke on one occasion and was paralyzed and unable to speak for a time. Fortunately, his speech and movement had both returned. However, he had started using drugs again and was very disappointed in himself. I told him that even though he had "fallen off the wagon," so to speak, God still loved him and he should never stop trying to be free of his addiction. All the time we were talking, nurses and therapists were coming into his room, making it difficult for us to talk. "This is just my luck," he said to me. "I finally get a visitor, and the nurses won't give us a chance to talk."

I handed him one of the prayers of Padre Pio, "Stay with me, Lord," and told him I would come back later in the afternoon. When I returned that afternoon, the young man looked much happier. He said he loved the prayer of Padre Pio so much that he had called his mother on the telephone and read it to her. The prayer had so touched him that he cried while reading it to his mother. He told her he was thinking that he should go back to the Catholic Church, which he had been away from for a long time. His mother told him she too would think about returning. After the phone call, he fell asleep, and he said he had not slept so peacefully and so deeply in a long time. I know that Padre Pio's prayers are powerful and transforming. I have seen it on many occasions. I thank God for the blessing of seeing that power working in that young man's heart that day.

Read

Faith is the realization of what is hoped for and evidence of things not seen.

—Hebrews 11:1

Reflect

You must not be discouraged or let yourself become dejected if your actions have not succeeded as perfectly as you intended. What do you expect? We are made of clay and not every soil yields the fruits expected by the one who tills it. But let us always humble ourselves and acknowledge that we are nothing if we lack the Divine assistance.

—Padre Pio

The "Stay with Me, Lord" prayer gave this young man the hope he needed to overcome his addiction and the ability to open his heart to the Lord and invite him back into his life. This was the moment when he was ready! The Lord was always present in him, but he needed to feel that presence. Once he did, he knew it was time to return to the one who loves him more than anyone else, the Lord! Once he knew he could return to the Lord, then he could ask the Lord to help him find his way out of this addiction.

The Lord is present in all of us all the time. Sometimes we forget he is there. There is no need to face those crises in our lives alone. Turn to the Lord, put it in his hands, and he will guide you. He will help you find the path that will take you to a new beginning.

Let Us Pray

Padre Pio, we pray you will stay close to us on this journey. We pray that we will arrive at Bethlehem with hearts full of hope, peace, joy, and love for the child Jesus!

Conclude your time of reflection and prayer with one Our Father, one Hail Mary, and one Glory Be.

DAY 15

A Phone Call and a Prayer

> It would be well to remember that the graces and consolations of prayer are not waters of this earth.
>
> —Padre Pio

During his lifetime, Padre Pio was attributed with a large number of miraculous cures. However, the miracles didn't end with his death. The following miracle occurred after the death of Padre Pio and is one of the miracles connected to his beatification.

While visiting with her widowed aunt on October 31, 1995, Signora Consiglia De Martino, a married woman with three children who lived in Salerno, Italy, began to feel a heavy pain in her chest and stomach, as if her insides were being turned around. She felt a malaise throughout her body, chills, and a sense of suffocation. She went to bed without supper and remained sleepless the entire night.

The following day, the pain persisted. Still Consiglia did her usual housework and even accompanied her daughter Daniela to school. Afterward, she was on her way to Mass when she felt increasingly ill and stopped instead at her sister's home. There she noticed the painful swelling of her neck and, looking in the mirror, perceived a lump as large as a grapefruit. She and her sister were very frightened, and they called Consiglia's husband to accompany them to the Riuniti Hospital in Salerno.

After ordering two CAT scans, the examining physician determined that Consiglia's thoracic duct in her neck had ruptured, forming the huge lump in her throat that contained approximately two liters of lymphatic fluid. Smaller deposits of fluid were causing the pain in her abdomen. Consiglia was told that she would need to undergo a very difficult and complicated surgical intervention as soon as possible. The surgery was scheduled for November 3.

Consiglia immediately began to pray to Padre Pio. She phoned his monastery at San Giovanni Rotondo, where she spoke with Fra Modestino Fucci—a brother to whom Padre Pio had promised to help with intercessory prayers. Fra Modestino prayed at the tomb of Padre Pio on November 1 and 2. During that time, physicians gave no medical treatment to Consiglia.

On November 2, Consiglia noticed a marked decrease in pain followed by a rapid diminution of the swelling in her neck. The following day, Consiglia was examined by physicians prior to her scheduled surgery. They immediately noticed the disappearance of the swelling in her neck and ordered X-rays of that area as well as her abdomen.

The X-rays showed the complete cure of the rupture of the thoracic duct that caused the lymphatic spilling, the complete disappearance of the liquid deposit in Consiglia's neck, and the complete disappearance of other liquid deposits in her abdomen.

The surgery was cancelled, and a CAT scan on November 6 confirmed the results of the X-rays taken on November 3: Consiglia had been immediately and inexplicably cured of a complex and dangerous condition—without any medical intervention whatsoever. She attributed the cure to Padre Pio to whom she, her family, and Fra Modestino had been praying. Successive examinations of Consiglia showed no long-term effects of her prior condition.

The diocesan investigation of the miracle took place from July 1996 to June 1997. Two ex officio experts and a medical consultant studied the published documentation and unanimously declared the "extraordinary and scientifically inexplicable nature of the cure." On April 30, 1998, the five-member medical committee of the Congregation for the Causes of Saints (CCS) at the Vatican declared unanimously that "the healing of the traumatically ruptured thoracic duct of Consiglia De Martino on November 3, 1995, is scientifically inexplicable." After the positive conclusion of the medical committee, the assembly of cardinal and bishop members of CCS approved the Consiglia De Martino case as a miracle on October 20, 1998.

Read

Rejoice always. Pray without ceasing. In all circumstances give thanks, for this is the will of God for you in Christ Jesus.

—1 Thessalonians 5:16–18

Reflect

I feel a great desire to abandon myself with greater trust to the Divine Mercy and to place my hope in God alone.

—Padre Pio

Let's reflect on the events that led to this immediate cure. Once the diagnosis was given, Consiglia immediately turned to Padre Pio. She called her friend Fra Modestino Fucci to pray for her to Padre Pio. On November 1, Fra Modestino went to the tomb of Padre Pio to pray for Consiglia. He continued to pray through the next day as well. During this time no medical treatment was given. It was Consiglia's prayers to Padre Pio that led to the cure.

In this miracle, the Lord shows us, as Padre Pio always tells us, that prayer is the answer. In this season of Advent, let us raise our voices in prayer and bring all our joys to the Christ Child in the manger.

Let Us Pray

Padre Pio, we pray you will stay close to us on this journey. We pray that we will arrive at Bethlehem with hearts full of hope, peace, joy, and love for the child Jesus!

Conclude your time of reflection and prayer with one Our Father, one Hail Mary, and one Glory Be.

Day 16

Padre Pio Talks with Jesus

How Jesus makes me happy! How gentle is His spirit!
But I get confused and can do nothing else than cry
and repeat, "Jesus, my bread!"

—Padre Pio

In October 1911, Padre Pio was sent to Venafro to study
sacred eloquence under the direction of his friend and
confessor Padre Agostino. While there, he became gravely
ill and was taken to Naples by the Father Superior, Padre
Evangelista, for a medical evaluation; however, the doctors didn't understand the nature of Padre Pio's illness
and were unable to help him. He was returned to Venafro
and confined to bed and was therefore unable to celebrate
Mass. Over the next twenty-one days, his only nourish-
ment was Holy Communion.

During this illness he had many ecstasies. Padre Agostino was an eyewitness of Padre Pio's ecstasies, and he
took it upon himself to jot down every word spoken by
Padre Pio. His penciled notes were written quickly. Afterward he copied everything in another notebook, which
eventually became the first part of his diary.

One morning, eight or nine days into his illness, Padre Pio was in a state of deep affliction after receiving Holy Communion. When asked the cause of his affliction, he responded, "Tell me the truth, did I receive Holy Communion this morning?"

The priest who had brought him Communion earnestly reassured him, but Padre Pio couldn't be persuaded. Finally, the priest directed a simple prayer to Padre Pio's guardian angel, and immediately Padre Pio remembered that he had received Communion and thanked the priest.

Padre Pio received Communion twice while he was in ecstasy, and it was Jesus who, during his ecstasy, made him aware of it, as the scribe reveals in his written record:

My Jesus . . . how wonderful You look this morning! . . . Tell me Jesus, are You in my heart? . . . Did I receive You this morning? . . . Yes? . . . And who was it that brought me Communion? . . . My papa? . . . It's always he who brings me Communion . . . if I ask him, he immediately responds: I gave you Holy Communion with these unworthy hands. . . . Ah Jesus, forgive me. . . . I already felt You in my heart like the disciples of Emmaus. . . . I felt You . . . with your sweetness. . . . I no longer feel thirsty. . . . Ah, my Jesus, my sweetness . . . how can I live without You? Come back always my Jesus, come, to You alone my heart belongs. . . . Oh, if I had infinite hearts, all the hearts in Heaven and on earth, even the heart of Your Mother, all of them, all of them I would offer them to You. . . . My Jesus, my

sweetness, Love, Love who sustains me . . . thank You
. . . to the next time![7]

Padre Pio's ecstasies happened two or three times a day
and lasted anywhere from one to two and a half hours.
Many doctors who tended to Padre Pio during his illness
witnessed these ecstasies. These doctors were amazed at
the sight of this phenomenon, at witnessing Padre Pio
speak directly with Jesus.

Read

And to know the love of Christ that surpasses knowledge, so that you may be filled with all the fullness of
God.

—Ephesians 3:19

Reflect

Without Jesus you can do nothing. In the end, the
gamble of our life is all in this Child. I live for Jesus
Christ, I live for his glory, I live to serve him, I live to
love him. In Jesus everything has an answer. Without
him—only a big void.

—Padre Pio

Can we imagine Jesus coming into our presence as he did
with Padre Pio? Can we imagine having long, beautiful
conversations with Jesus? Yes, we feel the presence of Jesus
after we receive Holy Communion, but to be able to speak
to Jesus as Padre Pio did would be amazing.

As we walk along this Advent path that will shortly bring us to Bethlehem, let us feel more closely the presence of the child Jesus. Let us speak in our hearts to Jesus and tell him we wish him to always remain in our hearts. Let us pray that when we meet him, he will come into our hearts and share his love with us as he did with Padre Pio in his ecstasies.

Let Us Pray

Padre Pio, we pray you will stay close to us on this journey. We pray that we will arrive at Bethlehem with hearts full of hope, peace, joy, and love for the child Jesus!

Conclude your time of reflection and prayer with one Our Father, one Hail Mary, and one Glory Be.

DAY 17

I Saw Padre Pio in a Dream

O how I need you, my Jesus, in this night of exile!
—Padre Pio

In 1999, Padre Pio was beatified. Just one year later, a miracle occurred that would lead to his canonization in 2002.

Matteo Pio Colella was just seven years old when he contracted a deadly disease. Doctors believed there was no hope for the boy. His cure was the miracle that paved the way for the canonization of St. Padre Pio by Pope John Paul II in June 2002. His name is St. Pio of Pietrelcina. People will always refer to him as Padre Pio, but this is the title that was bestowed on him by John Paul II.

On January 20, 2000, Matteo was diagnosed with acute fulminant meningitis, caused by bacteria. The disease had affected his kidneys, his respiratory system, and blood clotting. He was immediately admitted to the hospital founded by Padre Pio, the Home for the Relief of Suffering, located in San Giovanni Rotondo.

The following day, Matteo went into a coma. His health deteriorated drastically, and doctors thought he would die within a few hours. While Matteo was in this critical condition, his mother, Maria Lucia, went to pray over the tomb of Padre Pio to ask for her son's healing. Prior to Matteo Colella becoming ill, his mother had two dreams about Padre Pio:

> I found myself in the infirmary of the convent and I heard many people exclaiming, "Padre Pio is arriving; Padre Pio is arriving!" Then I experienced a very deep, unaccounted-for grief, and I knelt down shedding a flood of tears. Padre came close to me, and he gently said to me, "Why are you crying?" I replied, "I don't know why!" Then he caressed my cheek while pronouncing these words: "What are you afraid of? I am with you. I will always be near you!"
>
> Six or seven months later I had another dream that I was in a cemetery and Padre Pio came to me and asked me, "What are you doing here?" I replied with a shrug of my shoulders. Padre Pio smiled at me and said, "Walk on, move, get out of here, this is not for you! Be strong; you in front and I behind you, we will go away from here!"

While he was sick, Matteo also experienced Padre Pio's presence, which he later recounted:

> During the coma, I saw Padre Pio in a dream on my right and three angels on the left. One with golden wings and a white tunic and the two others with white wings and a red tunic.

Padre Pio, on my right, told me not to worry because I would soon be cured. In fact, my cure was like the resurrection of Lazarus.

And that's exactly what happened. The doctors considered Matteo to be clinically dead, but he came back to life.

When talking later about his experience, Matteo said, "I have always thought that I have received an enormous grace for which I must be thankful. When I talk to someone who doesn't believe, I tell him I'm here. For science it's inexplicable, but there is another explanation that we can't understand."

Read

So, the sisters sent word to him, saying, "Master, the one you love is ill."

—John 11:3

Reflect

Suffering, no matter how difficult it may be, when compared to the good that is accomplished, makes every pain a joy for the soul.

—Padre Pio

In Matteo's dream we see the "enormous grace for which I must be thankful" that Matteo mentions. What did the Lord have planned for Matteo? What did he save him for? We need to understand the enormity of this miracle: Matteo was, in essence, resurrected, as was Lazarus. He was clinically dead! And Matteo's miracle was used to canonize Padre Pio.

In this Advent season, as we look to Our Lord's greatest miracle, let us ponder on the enormity of the birth of Christ.

Let Us Pray

Padre Pio, we pray you will stay close to us on this journey. We pray that we will arrive at Bethlehem with hearts full of hope, peace, joy, and love for the child Jesus!

Conclude your time of reflection and prayer with one Our Father, one Hail Mary, and one Glory Be.

Day 18

My Eyes Were Dazzled by the Light

> May the Heavenly Child let your heart feel all those
> holy emotions that he allowed me to experience that
> blessed night when he was laid in that little hovel.
> Goodness, I could hardly express what I felt in my
> heart on that most happy night. My heart was over-
> flowing with holy love towards God made man.
> —Padre Pio

In this story, James Doyle tells us about a heavenly light
that appeared as his son was healed.

In May 1981, our thirteen-month-old-son Darren
became very ill with a high fever. My wife and I rushed
him to St. Joseph's Hospital in Clonmel (County Lim-
erick). He was diagnosed with bacterial meningitis.
By the time we got him to the hospital, he was only
semiconscious. The doctors were unable to set up an
IV for him because his veins had collapsed. A friend
of ours gave us a relic of Padre Pio and a Padre Pio
prayer card. We said the prayer many times a day at
Darren's bedside.

One day, I was sitting beside his bed saying the novena to Padre Pio. All of a sudden, my head was lifted toward the ceiling by a strange force under my chin. I saw what appeared to be a little blue light, no bigger than a flashlight bulb. My eyes were dazzled by this little light. It came down very slowly from the ceiling to the prayer card in my hand. It then shot from the prayer card into Darren's back. I told my wife, Barbara, what I had seen, but before she could ask me anything, Darren was moving, and he opened his eyes. For the first time in a week, he called out to us, "Mama, Daddy." He was released from the hospital one week later.

Read

Jesus spoke to them again, saying, "I am the light of the world. Whoever follows me will not walk in darkness, but will have the light of life."

—John 8:12

Reflect

Here these graceful little birds place their young ones, so that when the sea comes upon them by surprise, they can swim with confidence and float on the waves. . . . I want your heart to be like this: well compact and closed on all sides, so that if the worries and storms of the world, the evil spirit, and the flesh come upon it, it will not be penetrated. Leave but one opening to

your heart, that is toward heaven. . . . How I love and
am enraptured by those little birds.

—Padre Pio

What great faith these parents had! Mr. Doyle doesn't say
whether he knew of Padre Pio or if his friend's gift of the
relic and prayer card was the first time he'd heard of him.
What we do know is that he and his wife immediately
started to pray, and they continued to pray day and night
until their child was better.

When I read a story like this, I ask myself, *What do
people in difficult situations do when they don't have faith?*
It's frightening to think about.

Was the force under Mr. Doyle's chin that made him
look up in amazement at the light that shot from above
to the prayer card and to his son's back the Light of the
world? Was this light Jesus Christ? Is Jesus saying through
this story that when you're in trouble, turn toward the
light and he will be there to help you?

Do you turn to the light when you are scared or
troubled?

Today let us think about Jesus, the Light of the world.
Are you dazzled by the light? You should be! You should
search every day of your life for this light of hope, of
peace, of joy, and of love. This light has led you along this
path to Bethlehem. Soon you will be in the presence of
the child Jesus, the Light of the world. Be prepared to be
dazzled by his presence.

Let Us Pray

Padre Pio, we pray you will stay close to us on this journey. We pray that we will arrive at Bethlehem with hearts full of hope, peace, joy, and love for the child Jesus!

Conclude your time of reflection and prayer with one Our Father, one Hail Mary, and one Glory Be.

$\bigcirc$AY 19

$\top$ish and Chips and Padre Pio

As the days pass, I see ever more clearly the greatness of God, and in this light, which grows brighter and brighter, my soul burns with the desire to be united to him by indissoluble bonds.

—Padre Pio

Michael Gromley tells about the miraculous healing of his daughter:

My daughter Elizabeth was eight years old when she was diagnosed with Hodgkin's disease. She stayed at Our Lady's Children's Hospital in Dublin for a number of weeks. I used to visit her on my lunch break every day and also at the end of my workday. Her throat was affected by the disease, and she lost the ability to speak. One day a nun, who was the head nurse on my daughter's ward, pulled me aside to speak to me privately. She told me that Elizabeth was not going to survive the cancer. After she told me that, I went to the Capuchin Friary at St. Mary of the Angels in Dublin. One of the Capuchins, Fr. John, had a glove of Padre Pio's. I have had a devotion to Padre Pio for many years, and I asked him to visit Elizabeth and bless her with it.

Fr. John came to the hospital and blessed Elizabeth with the glove as well as all of the other children. Not long after, I was having a meal at the fish and chips restaurant on Kimmage Road in Dublin. Suddenly, the whole area was pervaded with the fragrance of roses. I instantly knew it was Padre Pio, even though I thought it was an odd place for him to make his presence known. A few days later, I spoke to the head nurse again. She told me that she had astounding news: all of Elizabeth's tests were normal.

My daughter recovered rapidly and completely, and her voice came back full strength. When she got older, she sang professionally throughout Europe. I believe that through the intercession of Padre Pio, my daughter was healed.

Read

But you, Bethlehem-Ephrathah least among the clans of Judah, From you shall come forth for me one who is to be ruler in Israel; Whose origin is from of old, from ancient times.

—Micah 5:1

Reflect

I no sooner begin to pray than my soul becomes enveloped in a peace and tranquility that words cannot describe.

—Padre Pio

Mr. Gromley came into the presence of Padre Pio in the most peculiar place: a fish and chips restaurant. He received a great sign, one that so many receive when they are in the presence of Padre Pio: the fragrance of roses. Think of what Mr. Gromley said: "The whole area was pervaded with the fragrance of roses. I instantly knew it was Padre Pio." No hesitation!

Mr. Gromley had great faith that, through the intercession of Padre Pio, his daughter Elizabeth would be healed. Not only was she cured, but also, even though her throat was affected by the disease, she went on to become a singer, performing throughout Europe. God had a plan. Just as God has a plan for all of us.

Today, think about God's plan for you. What is it he is asking you to do? Think about a great crisis in your life. How many times when we have a crisis in our lives do we ask, "What have you saved me for, dear Lord?" What is it he needs you to do for him?

We are now approaching Bethlehem. Very soon we will be kneeling at the manger. What will we say to the child Jesus? Will we ask him why he wanted us on this journey and what he needs from us? Open up your hearts and listen to the voice of the child calling you to Bethlehem.

Let Us Pray

Padre Pio, we pray you will stay close to us on this journey. We pray that we will arrive at Bethlehem with hearts full of hope, peace, joy, and love for the child Jesus!

Conclude your time of reflection and prayer with one Our Father, one Hail Mary, and one Glory Be.

Day 20

Our Lady Entrusted an Unborn Child to Brother Pio!

There is an urgency, a grave danger, a soul or a body to save.

—Padre Pio

Of all the miracles associated with Padre Pio, this is the most important because Our Lady was present at this miracle, and she instructed Padre Pio on how he would lead this child through an exemplary life. She entrusted Padre Pio with this child before she was born. She also prepared Padre Pio for his role in the future. As Our Lady of Guadalupe is the patroness of the unborn, by this miracle, Padre Pio would become the patron of the unborn.

On January 18, 1905, while Pio, then a young monk, was praying at the monastery of St. Elia in Piansi, he was miraculously transported to the garden of a mansion in Udine. Giovanni Battista Rizzani, the father of the family who lived there, was on his deathbed, and Leonilde, the mother, was about to give birth to Giovanna. Leonilde came outside to quiet the howling dogs. There, in the garden, she went into labor and delivered her baby.

Whenever Leonilde reminisced about that memorable day, she always said she had seen a young Capuchin at Giovanna's birth. And Brother Pio reported to his spiritual director that he had mysteriously witnessed the birth. He said the Virgin Mary had appeared to him, entrusted Giovanna to him, and instructed him to polish her until she shone beautifully. "She will seek you out," said Mary, "but first you will meet her in St. Peter's."

Seventeen years later, Giovanna, full of doubts about her faith, went to St. Peter's Basilica looking for a priest who might help her. A sacristan told her that the basilica was about to close and no priests were available, but then a Capuchin seemed to appear from nowhere. He welcomed her into his confessional and provided satisfying answers to some of the questions that bedeviled her. Giovanna waited outside to greet the priest, but he never came out, disappearing as quietly as he had arrived.

One day during the following summer, she learned about Padre Pio, and a few days later she followed a compelling desire to seek him out at Santa Maria delle Grazie, his monastery. Giovanna stood in a crowd hoping to see him. As he walked by, he stopped in front of her and startled her by saying, "Giovanna, I know you. You were born the day your father died."

The next morning Giovanna went to Padre Pio for confession. "Daughter," he said, "at last you have come to me. I have been waiting for you for a long time."

"Father, you must be mistaken," said Giovanna. "This is my first time at San Giovanni Rotondo."

"No, I am making no mistake," he said. "Last summer at St. Peter's you asked a Capuchin priest to help you with your doubts about your faith. I was that priest."

Then Giovanna recognized him.

"When you were being born, the Virgin Mary took me to your home. I witnessed your birth in the garden. Mary entrusted you to my care and made me responsible to help you grow in holiness. She told me that someday I would meet you at St. Peter's."

These revelations touched Giovanna dramatically, and she became his spiritual daughter. A few years later, he had her join the Franciscan Third Order. Customarily, new members of the order had to choose a new name, and Padre Pio gave her the unusual name "Jacoba."

"What an ugly name," said Giovanna. "I don't like it."

"You will be called Sister Jacoba," he explained, "because like Jacoba, the noble Roman friend who was present at the death of St. Francis, you will be present at my death."

In the early morning of September 23, 1968, Giovanna had a mysterious vision in which she was transported to Padre Pio's cell, where she witnessed his death. Later, when she told one of the monks about it, she accurately described the saint's cell, which she had never visited, and named those who were attending him in his final hour.

Giovanna remained a devoted disciple of Padre Pio and gave a detailed deposition before the Archiepiscopal Curia of Manfredonia for the cause of beatification. The curia compared her document to that written by Padre Pio in 1905 and noted the similarities. The document of Padre Pio was never read by Giovanna, and Padre Pio's bilocation was known, up to that time, only by his superiors.

Read

For we walk by faith, not by sight.

—2 Corinthians 5:7

Reflect

Give yourself up into the arms of your Heavenly Mother. She will take good care of your soul.

—Padre Pio

Our Lady instructed the young Brother Pio to care for Giovanna. These words really confused Brother Pio because he was a young monk, not yet a priest, and very poor. How could he possibly take care of this child?

Our Lady took Padre Pio to the garden of the Rizzini home because she wanted him to witness the birth of Giovanna. By witnessing the birth of this child, Padre Pio would be witnessing the birth of all the unborn. He would understand that he must be a champion of life—not just Giovanna's life but the life of all unborn babies.

Padre Pio has always been very outspoken when it comes to the life of a child, especially the unborn child who has no one to speak for them.

Let Us Pray

Padre Pio, we pray you will stay close to us on this journey. We pray that we will arrive at Bethlehem with hearts full of hope, peace, joy, and love for the child Jesus!

Conclude your time of reflection and prayer with one Our Father, one Hail Mary, and one Glory Be.

Day 21

Lucia and the Crucifix

Humility is truth; truth is humility.

—Padre Pio

In one her of diaries, Mary Pyle, assistant to Padre Pio, speaks of a letter written by Lucia Fiorentino, a mystic who lived from 1889 to 1934. In 1906, at the age of seventeen, Lucia had a vision in which she predicted the arrival of Padre Pio in San Giovanni Rotondo. When he arrived, Lucia became one of his spiritual daughters. This is Lucia's vision:

> I saw in a vision a tree of immeasurable size in the atrium of our Capuchin Friary and heard a voice which said to me: "This is a symbol of a soul which is now far away but will come to [you] and do much good in this town. . . . He will be strong and well rooted as this tree, and all souls which come to him—those of the town and elsewhere—if they take refuge in its shade, will be freed from evil [that is, who comes to this priest to be enlightened, to find pardon and a remedy for their faults]. If they humble themselves, they will receive counsel and fruit for eternal life from this

worthy priest. Those who despise his counsel, his way of doing things, will be punished by the Lord in this life and in the next. His mission will go around the world. Many will take refuge in the shade of this mystical tree so as to have fruits of grace and forgiveness."[8]

After sharing Lucia's vision, Mary continued with a story about Lucia Fiorentino and a crucifix. At the time, there lived in San Giovanni Rotondo an old woman who was poor, blind, and partly deaf. There was nothing in her life that could cheer her or from which she could obtain comfort except a small crucifix Padre Pio had sent to her through Lucia Fiorentino, who felt sorry for the woman. The small crucifix was constantly in her hands, and she would cover it with kisses when she went to bed at night. The woman called it her "Padre Pio's Jesus Christ."

One evening the old woman began to weep and wail. "I have lost my Padre Pio's Jesus Christ! How can I go to sleep without my crucifix?" She called in her neighbors, who tried to comfort her. Her friends searched the house looking everywhere but could not find the crucifix. The woman's niece came to sleep with her as usual, but there was no sleep for the poor woman that evening; her heart was too heavy over the loss of her one and only treasure. At about two o'clock the next morning, the woman thought the front door had been opened. She felt a gush of wind and then the presence of someone near her. Suddenly she felt an object being placed in her hand. The door closed, and she was alone again. Her niece slept quietly at her side. Slowly she opened her hand and there saw the crucifix. Quietly, she said to herself, "Padre Pio has brought back my crucifix."

As soon as it was light, the old woman sent for Lucia and told her what had happened. Lucia's amazement knew no bounds, for the crucifix wasn't the original one but rather a new one—or at least a different one—the type of which Padre Pio had been giving away at the time. Lucia hastened up to the monastery and asked Padre Pio if he had given the old woman the crucifix. Padre Pio merely replied, "She has her crucifix. Well, that suffices."

Read

Rejoice in the Lord always.

—Philippians 4:4

Reflect

Have great confidence in God's goodness and mercy, and he will never abandon you; but don't neglect to embrace his holy cross because of this.

—Padre Pio

When Lucia first met Padre Pio she said, "I had the good fortune to confer alone with Padre Pio in the sacristy. I felt beside myself and as if I were truly in the presence of Jesus. My soul was full of brim [joy] and I had all the energy to open up my heart to him and reveal the necessities of my conscience. . . . I felt as if I were in Paradise."[9]

On this road to Bethlehem, let us reveal the necessities of our conscience to Padre Pio, who is always at the side of the Christ Child.

Let Us Pray

Padre Pio, we pray you will stay close to us on this journey. We pray that we will arrive at Bethlehem with hearts full of hope, peace, joy, and love for the child Jesus!

Conclude your time of reflection and prayer with one Our Father, one Hail Mary, and one Glory Be.

Day 22

The Man in the Trench Coat

> In darkness, at times of tribulation and distress of the spirit, Jesus is with you. In such a state you see nothing but darkness, but I can assure you on God's behalf that the light of the Lord is all around you and pervades your spirit.
>
> —Padre Pio

On March 14, 1988, Dora Silva, her husband Silvano, and their daughter Kimberly were involved in a car accident in San Antonio, Texas. Two-year-old Kimberly sustained severe head injuries. She was transferred to the trauma center at Brooke Army Hospital in San Antonio. Silvano had a cut on his left arm, and Dora sustained a mild head concussion that caused double vision. About that experience, Dora shares:

> The morning after the accident, a wonderful friend of mine, Connie Zamora, showed up at the hospital and brought me a Padre Pio prayer card with a relic. She said she had heard about our accident on the radio. I thought it was strange because I didn't recall radio stations releasing names, but I dismissed that puzzle

to tell Connie I had never heard of Padre Pio. She said that, before we started the Efficacious Novena to the Sacred Heart of Jesus, we should place the relic on Kimberly's forehead and her index finger. She said that if my prayers were answered, someone would tell me a man came to visit our daughter to heal her. I told her we were always at the hospital. She said, "Have faith."

My mom and dad were with my husband and me in the ICU for three weeks. We prayed the Padre Pio prayer novena all day long, taking turns praying.

Kimberly had severe head injuries; she was paralyzed on her left side, and her left pupil was fixed. She started having seizures about six days after the accident. The doctors said they might have to do surgery to relieve some of the pressure on her brain. The doctor ordered an MRI to see what was going on in her brain. When the neurologist came to give my husband and me the MRI results, she raised up her sleeve and said she had goosebumps on her arms because she could not believe what she saw. She said Kimberly was stable and all they needed to do was increase her seizure medication; they wouldn't need to do surgery. Kimberly was still in critical condition but stable.

It was about midnight when the doctor told us to go home and get some rest. The doctor and my parents convinced my husband and me to go home. The next morning when we arrived, the nurse told my husband and me that a man in a trench coat came to see our daughter in the middle of the night. Since my family is from San Antonio, I didn't think too much about a man visiting my daughter at that time.

Every day after that the doctor said he didn't know if Kimberly would ever be normal again. It wasn't until the third week that Kimberly started responding to treatment. She opened up her eyes. We were excited, but we still feared the unknown, whether she would be able to walk, talk, and be normal again. One day Kimberly raised her right arm and started patting her leg. We called the nurse, in fear of seizures, but they weren't seizures. We continued to try to figure out what she was trying to communicate to us. I asked her if she needed to go potty, and when we took her to the bathroom, she went potty! I knew then that her memory was there. The recovery and healing that began from that point was amazing.

As Kimberly's health improved, she was able to be transferred from the ICU to Santa Rosa's Children's Hospital in downtown San Antonio. When she was in San Antonio, my friend Connie came to visit Kimberly again. This time she brought Kimberly a "miracle balloon." During her visit, Connie reached over and tapped the balloon on Kimberly's leg. After being tapped a few times, Kimberly moved her left side and kicked the balloon using her left leg, which until then had been paralyzed.

We thanked Padre Pio for his intercession and for the healing. Going through this experience helped me realize how we take life for granted and when it's almost taken away it puts things in perceptive. As Kimberly took steps in her recovery, we were so excited and grateful.

Eventually, we were allowed to take Kimberly home to continue her recovery and work on her physical therapy. We also had to take her to an eye specialist for treatment, as Kimberly was having problems with the optic nerve in her left eye, which caused her eye to wander. The specialist was concerned this would cause her to lose her eyesight in her left eye. When patching her right eye to force her to use, and hopefully strengthen, her left eye didn't work, the specialist said there was an experimental injection he thought would help correct the optic nerves. We went back to the specialist the day before the procedure for the doctor to dilate her eyes and examine her again. The doctor was shocked; the examination showed that Kimberly's optic nerve had corrected itself and she did not need the injection procedure.

When we first came home from the hospital, I was so scared for Kimberly to fall asleep. I feared she wouldn't wake up. However, as time passed, I started to think about and replay in my mind everything that happened since the accident. It was at that time that I realized all of the blessings and miracles Kimberly had received. Then my husband shared with me what happened the night of the accident.

While waiting for the ambulance, my husband told me, a man showed up in a trench coat. The man approached the car, took his trench coat off, and covered Kimberly with it. My husband said he didn't know what happened to the man as he didn't see him after that. Then we remembered the man that showed up in a trench coat to see Kimberly when she was in the ICU.

I asked my family if anyone had gone to visit Kimberly in the middle of the night and everyone said no.

As we reflected on all that happened since that night, we realized that Padre Pio was at the scene of the accident covering Kimberly with his trench coat; he showed up at the hospital to heal her when she was in the ICU. Padre Pio had surely interceded before the injection procedure for her eye, and Kimberly was healed.

As Kimberly was growing up, I would tell her someday we would visit Padre Pio to say thank you. We were able to do this in 2008, when we had the wonderful opportunity to travel on a pilgrimage to Italy and visit the tomb of Padre Pio at San Giovanni Rotando. Months before our pilgrimage, Susan at Little Flower Pilgrimages notified me that Padre Pio's body was going to be exhumed and we would be able to see Padre Pio when we visited San Giovanni Rotondo. My husband, Kimberly, and I were able to say thank you to Padre Pio in person for all of the miracles he sent our beautiful and healthy daughter.

Read

Whatever you ask for in prayer with faith, you will receive.

—Matthew 21:22

Reflect

Once I take on a soul, I also take on the entire family
as my spiritual children.

—Padre Pio

The amazing thing about this miracle was that Dora and
Silvano had no idea who Padre Pio was, but they had faith
that through his intercession their daughter, Kimberly,
would be cured.

Padre Pio was with them at the scene of the accident,
even before they knew who he was. Did Padre Pio recognize the great faith of these people? Why did he help them
when they didn't even know he existed? I think he knew
their faith was so great that they would spend the rest of
their lives promoting Padre Pio's message and thanking
the Lord for sending Padre Pio to them.

As we look toward Christ's birth, the outcome of
Mary's trusting yes, we can see a similar strong faith in
the Silvas' story. Do you have such unconditional faith?

Let Us Pray

Padre Pio, we pray you will stay close to us on this journey.
We pray that we will arrive at Bethlehem with hearts full
of hope, peace, joy, and love for the child Jesus!

*Conclude your time of reflection and prayer with one Our
Father, one Hail Mary, and one Glory Be.*

Day 23

Any Friend of Padre Pio Is a Friend of Mine

> You see yourself forsaken and I assure you that Jesus is holding you tighter than ever to his divine Heart.
> —Padre Pio

This is a beautiful story that Patti Karlton tells us about a waitress, a single mother with a young son who was in need of an apartment and had very limited funds:

Once, when my daughter and I were having dinner at one of our favorite restaurants, I fell into a conversation with our waitress. She told me how tough her life was. She was a single parent and in urgent need of a new place for her and her young son to live. She worked long hours at the diner trying to save her money for a decent place to live. I asked her if she had ever heard of Padre Pio; when she said that she had not, I wrote his name down and told her to read about him online and then to pray to him for help. About five months later I returned to the restaurant. "Oh, thank God you are here," I heard the waitress say as I walked into the diner. She then gave me a hug and said to me,

"I have been hoping you would return because I want to share my miracle of Padre Pio with you!"

The waitress told me that after reading about Padre Pio she prayed to him as I had suggested. After she had saved enough money, she began to look for a small house to rent. Her mother allowed her and her son to move in with her until she found a place. She found one place that she liked very much, but when she found out the rent was two thousand dollars a month, she became sad. "I am sorry I bothered you," she said to the owner of the home. "I didn't realize the rent was so expensive. I cannot afford it. I have prayed so hard to Padre Pio to help me." "How do you know about Padre Pio?" the owner of the house asked. Then she explained how I came to the restaurant and talked to her about Padre Pio. The owner asked her how much she could afford for rent, and she told her that seven hundred dollars a month was her limit. "Then that is the price it will be, because any friend of Padre Pio is a friend of mine!" the owner said to her.

Read

Then call on me on the day of distress; I will rescue you, and you shall honor me.

—Psalm 50:15

Reflect

I feel a great desire to abandon myself with greater
trust to the Divine Mercy and to place my hope in
God alone.

—Padre Pio

Faith can move mountains! Think of the faith of this
waitress. She had never heard of Padre Pio, but when she
began to read about him, she had faith that he would help
her find the house she needed. And how about the person
who allowed her to rent the house for only seven hundred
dollars? What an amazingly generous person, one whose
generosity was inspired by his faith.

This story reminds us that there are really good people in this world, and when we have faith and trust in the
Lord, he will always listen to our prayers.

As we reflect on our hearts and actions to prepare for
the coming of Our Lord this Advent, do we see times we
have helped our neighbors in need? Have we shared our
good fortune with them? Perhaps we should think about
those who are less fortunate than us. Do they need shelter,
as the Christ Child did at his birth? Do they need to find
their way to a safe haven? Can we help them to get there?
How does our faith, and our friendship with saints such
as Padre Pio, inspire us to be generous?

Let Us Pray

Padre Pio, we pray you will stay close to us on this journey. We pray that we will arrive at Bethlehem with hearts full of hope, peace, joy, and love for the child Jesus!

Conclude your time of reflection and prayer with one Our Father, one Hail Mary, and one Glory Be.

Day 24

I Held the Relic Over My Eyes

Prayer is the oxygen of the soul.

—Padre Pio

Claudia Bartoli-McKinney tells the story of how her grandfather encouraged her to pray:

My grandfather George Bartoli went to see Padre Pio twice in his life. In 1957, he was able to make his confession to Padre Pio. Usually confessions to Padre Pio lasted just a few minutes, but after the confession, Padre Pio and my grandfather talked for a long time. Padre Pio seemed happy to speak with him and was in no hurry to end the conversation. My grandfather had a handkerchief with him of a friend who was dying of cancer. In addition to the many other things they talked about—including the wine and good food of the region of Italy my grandfather was from—he spoke to Padre Pio about her. "She will be in paradise soon," Padre Pio said. Then he blessed the handkerchief, saying that perhaps it would comfort her. My grandfather had always been a worrier. "Stay calm," Padre Pio repeated to him over and over.

It was through my grandfather's love for Padre Pio, a love that was only reaffirmed by the comfort Padre Pio had given him for his dying friend, that I came to know and love him as well. I had drifted away from my Catholic faith and had become involved in the New Age movement. My husband and I separated and then divorced. I was living alone with my daughter, and I was depressed. During all of this, my grandfather prayed very hard for me to return to my faith. Then I began to have double vision, then blurry vision, and finally no vision at all. I was ready to get a seeing-eye dog. The doctor thought I had had a stroke, but later I was diagnosed with myasthenia gravis, a neuromuscular disease. The muscles in my eyelids became so weak that I could not even hold them open. I was set to have an operation on my eyes, but there was no guarantee that my sight would be restored.

My grandfather drove me to a final doctor appointment before the surgery. He gave me a relic of Padre Pio and told me to pray to him. I went into the examination room, and before the doctor came in, I held the relic over my eyes and prayed and begged Padre Pio to heal me. My grandfather was in the waiting room, praying for me. The doctor examined my eyes and then left the room. He came back, examined them one more time, and then left the room again. He came in a third time with another doctor who also examined my eyes. Then they both left. I was quite scared. The doctor came in once again and told me that he wanted to cancel my surgery because he believed I did not need the operation. I began to get my vision back. The biggest miracle of all was that because of the healing of my eyes, my faith was restored and also my marriage. My husband and I reconciled and were reunited after being apart for more than five years.

Read

He blinded their eyes and hardened their heart, so that they might not see with their eyes and understand with their heart and be converted, and I would heal them.

—John 12:40

Reflect

Remember: the sinner who is sorry for his sins is closer to God than the just man who boasts of his good works.

—Padre Pio

When we are separated from God, we lose sight of what is good and important to us. When we disobey God and begin to serve ourselves, we become spiritually blind. Left to our own devices, humans are spiritually blinded and without hope. But Jesus, the Light of the world, can open our eyes to see. Through Christ we receive spiritual sight!

In order for Claudia to see the error of her ways, she needed to be physically blinded. Once she put her faith back in God, her physical and spiritual sight was restored and so were other important parts of her life.

Are we spiritually blinded by our everyday lives that are so demanding? On this journey of Advent, let us keep our eyes wide open so we may see the Christ Child in everything we do.

Let Us Pray

Padre Pio, we pray you will stay close to us on this journey. We pray that we will arrive at Bethlehem with hearts full of hope, peace, joy, and love for the child Jesus!

Conclude your time of reflection and prayer with one Our Father, one Hail Mary, and one Glory Be.

Day 25

A Visit from Padre Pio

Our present life is given only to gain the eternal one
and if we don't think about it, we build our affections
on what belongs to this world, where our life is tran-
sitory. When we have to leave it we are afraid and
become agitated. Believe me, to live happily in this
pilgrimage, we have to aim at the hope of arriving at
our Homeland, where we will stay eternally.

—Padre Pio

In 1975, Marge Spada's husband, Joe, was hospitalized
with terminal cancer. Up to the time of her husband's
hospitalization, Marge had never heard of Padre Pio. Then
a friend gave her a book for Joe to read on the life of
Padre Pio, the Capuchin priest who bore the stigmata,
the crucifixion wounds of Christ. Joe read the book. He
was so impressed that he began to pray to Padre Pio. Then
unexpected things began to happen!

On several occasions, when Joe's nurses came into
his room, they were overcome by the beautiful aroma of
fresh flowers. They couldn't understand where the aroma
was coming from, as there were no flowers in the room.

Pope John Paul II calls the aroma of Padre Pio "the aroma of sanctity." This aroma to some people is the sweet smell of tobacco; to others, it is the aroma of fresh flowers. When one smells this aroma of Padre Pio, he is telling you he is with you, and he was with Joe in his hospital room, even though the nurses did not realize it.

Joe told Marge that frequently, Padre Pio would walk up and down the halls of the hospital with him. On one particular night, Marge arrived at the hospital, and as she sat down beside Joe, he said, "Marge, Padre Pio was here just a short time ago, and he was sitting where you are sitting."

As Joe was telling Marge of Padre Pio's visit, her eyes fell on a handkerchief that she did not recognize. As she reached for it, Joe said, "That's Padre Pio's handkerchief. He put it there on the stand just before he left."

Padre Pio made many visits to Joe at the hospital, by aroma and through bilocation. Joe was not healed of cancer, but his last days were peaceful, living proof of Padre Pio's promise to be with those who pray to him or call upon him for assistance. Padre Pio did not abandon Marge either in her time of need. After the funeral, although it was a frosty autumn day, visitors who arrived at her home said they could smell the aroma of fresh flowers outside surrounding her home. And Marge tells that on several occasions, Padre Pio's handkerchief has given off the aroma of fresh flowers.

On Joe's tombstone, Marge had carved, "Joe had a vision of Padre Pio."

Marge's love for Padre Pio and her desire to share him with everyone led her to found the Padre Pio Foundation of America. To her last day on earth, Marge felt the presence of Padre Pio through the gift of perfume, and she knew he was with her in her prayers. She went to her eternal home on Christmas Eve, 2011. Her last days continued to be filled with spreading devotion to Padre Pio at the hospital, as her husband had once done for her in his hospital.

Read

With firm purpose you maintain peace; in peace, because of our trust in you.

—Isaiah 26:3

Reflect

The heart of our Divine Master has no more amiable law than that of sweetness, humility, charity. Often place your confidence in Divine Providence and be assured that sooner heaven and earth shall pass away than that the Lord neglect to protect you.

—Padre Pio

In Padre Pio's book, Joe found not the miracles but the simplicity of the man. He saw a humble man who spent his entire life in the service of the Lord. I don't think Joe ever asked for or expected a miracle from Padre Pio, yet he still experienced the gift of Padre Pio's presence.

Could you imagine what it was like for Joe to spend his last days on earth in the presence of Padre Pio? Together they prepared for Joe's arrival in paradise. I have no doubt that Padre Pio was waiting at the gates of heaven for Joe and then for Marge, gates that Jesus opened to us through his Death and Resurrection.

Let Us Pray

Padre Pio, we pray you will stay close to us on this journey. We pray that we will arrive at Bethlehem with hearts full of hope, peace, joy, and love for the child Jesus!

Conclude your time of reflection and prayer with one Our Father, one Hail Mary, and one Glory Be.

Day 26

Bring Your Little Girl Here to Me in Italy

I feel a great desire to abandon myself with greater trust to the Divine Mercy and to place my hope in God alone.

—Padre Pio

In April 1966, Vera and Harry Calandra were thrilled to welcome their fifth child into the world. But Vera Marie, born with congenital defects of the urinary tract, was ultimately not expected to live beyond her first year.

After all medical hope had been given up, the Calandras relied even more heavily on their faith. After being introduced to the life of Padre Pio through reading a book, Vera began to experience signs that her prayers for her daughter were being heard. Padre Pio began making his presence known to her, first through the fragrance of roses and then by distinct locution: "Bring your little girl here to me in Italy, and do not delay; come immediately."

Encouraged by her husband, Harry, Vera obediently listened to Padre Pio's call. With her oldest child, Michael, newborn Christina, and now two-year-old Vera Marie in tow, Vera traveled from the United States to San Giovanni Rotondo, Italy, to meet the "priest who worked miracles." The young mother was granted two audiences with Padre Pio, during which he blessed her and her children, placing his sore, wounded hands on their heads. While in the presence of the future saint, Vera kissed his hand and spoke to him through her heart: "Please God, make a miracle so that all the people will believe." She made a silent promise to Almighty God that if her daughter were to live, the whole world would know the greatness of Padre Pio.

Vera's prayers were answered: upon returning home with Vera Marie, her doctors discovered what they described as a "rudimentary bladder" growing in place of the one that had been removed during an earlier medical intervention. Vera Marie's health improved greatly, her prognosis was strong, and Vera kept the promise she made to God in Italy. The Calandras devoted their lives to bringing souls to God through the intercession of Padre Pio, eventually founding the National Centre for Padre Pio in 1971. Today, Vera Marie serves as the center's assistant manager and vice president, working alongside two of her sisters and several of her nieces and nephews to lead the center into a future of growth.

Read

You have given me health and restored my life!
—Isaiah 38:16

Reflect

Pray, hope, and don't worry. Worry is useless. God is
merciful and will hear your prayer.

—Padre Pio

It's interesting that Padre Pio reached out to Vera Calandra and not the other way around. She had only heard about Padre Pio through his life story. After the doctors told Vera that Vera Marie would not live to be one year old, she began to put her faith in God. And how did God answer? Through Padre Pio.

Padre Pio was calling Vera. He was begging her, "Don't delay; come immediately!" Why was Padre Pio doing this? Why was he calling her to come immediately? Was he testing her faith? Was he asking her to put it all in the hands of God? He was asking her to take her very sick child and travel thousands of miles to Italy where he would be waiting for her. Any mother would think twice before she would make such a journey with a very sick child, but Vera never hesitated. She trusted that the Lord would protect her child on this journey and make her well. She took Vera Marie and two of her other children and traveled to San Giovanni Rotondo.

There were other forces at work here too. Vera didn't just take Vera Marie and then walk away thankful; no, she made a promise to the Lord: "Please God, make a miracle so that all people will believe." She put her trust in God, and God entrusted her to spread the word about Padre Pio.

On this Advent journey, let us answer the call of Padre Pio to follow him to Bethlehem to the manger, where we know the Christ Child is waiting for us. Let us answer this call of Padre Pio: "Don't delay; come immediately."

Let Us Pray

Padre Pio, we pray you will stay close to us on this journey. We pray that we will arrive at Bethlehem with hearts full of hope, peace, joy, and love for the child Jesus!

Conclude your time of reflection and prayer with one Our Father, one Hail Mary, and one Glory Be.

$\int$AY 27

$\int$o Not Say Anything to Anyone

Stay very close to the crib of this most beautiful Child.
—Padre Pio

Padre Pio loved the privilege of celebrating midnight Mass in the sixteenth-century church of Santa Maria delle Grazie in San Giovanni Rotondo. Since this was a solemn Mass, the privilege of celebrating it would have normally been reserved for the guardian of the monastery, but knowing how dear that particular Mass was to Padre Pio, the guardians always allowed him to celebrate it. This celebration made a profound impression on those fortunate enough to attend.

The road to the church was a rocky path that led from the city to the friary, and in winter, it was almost always covered in ice and snow. Even so, many people would undertake the journey and wait for hours in order to attend Padre Pio's Christmas Eve Mass. His Christmas Eve Mass was long, sometimes only finishing at five o'clock in the morning.

Before Mass, Padre Pio would greet those attending, and his face would already seem to be transfigured.

On the evening of December 24, 1922, many people arrived early to attend Padre Pio's Christmas Eve midnight Mass. While they waited for Mass to begin, Lucia Ladanza, a spiritual daughter of Padre Pio, and three other women prayed the Rosary. Lucia recalled a miraculous event that took place that evening:

> The friars had brought in a huge brazier to keep the gathering warm. The three women praying with Lucia had all dozed off with the warmth of the stove. From the inner stairway of the sacristy, Padre Pio descended and halted by the window. Suddenly, the child Jesus appeared in a halo of light and rested in Padre Pio's arms; then Padre Pio's face became radiant. When the vision ended, Padre Pio noticed that Lucia was awake and looking at him astonished. He went up to her and asked, "Lucia, what did you see?" Lucia answered, "Padre Pio, I saw everything." Padre Pio replied, "Do not say anything to anyone."

We do not know how Padre Pio himself felt in those moments. He was very reserved and guarded his spiritual life closely. In addition, Padre Pio was always a humble and reserved friar. He considered himself the least among his brothers. Perhaps his feelings when holding the Christ Child can be explained in his private correspondence to his confessor: "May the Heavenly Child let your heart feel all those holy emotions that he allowed me to experience that blessed night when he was laid in that little hovel. Goodness, I could hardly express what I felt in my heart on that most happy night. My heart was overflowing with holy love towards God made man."[10]

Read

She gave birth to a son, a male child, destined to rule all the nations with an iron rod. Her child was caught up to God and to his throne.

—Revelation 12:5

Reflect

Nothing can be heard except the sobs and whimpers of the infant God. And by means of his crying and weeping he offers to the Divine justice the first ransom for our redemption.

—Padre Pio

What would you do if you suddenly saw the child Jesus appear? You know he's always there, but what if he decided to show himself? Are you ready to meet him? What would you say to him? Would you be worried about what he would say to you? The only answer is to always be prepared.

Tomorrow is Christmas Eve! This is the perfect opportunity to prepare to meet the child Jesus, to open your heart to him, and to let him know how sorry you are for all the times you've disappointed him by your sins.

Remember, Jesus has a short memory. As soon as we ask for forgiveness for our sins, Jesus forgets them. They are gone forever.

As part of this Advent journey, let us make a good examination of conscience and confess our sins so we will be able to meet the child Jesus at Bethlehem with a pure and opened heart.

Let Us Pray

Padre Pio, we pray you will stay close to us on this journey. We pray that we will arrive at Bethlehem with hearts full of hope, peace, joy, and love for the child Jesus!

Conclude your time of reflection and prayer with one Our Father, one Hail Mary, and one Glory Be.

$\mathcal{D}$AY 28

Tonight, Heaven Opened!

The Heavenly Child suffers and cries in the crib so as to make His suffering for us loveable, meritorious and sought after. He lacked everything so that we might learn from him to renounce earthly goods. He was pleased with humble and poor adorers so that we might love poverty and prefer the company of the little and simple ones to those of the great of the world. . . . With His birth he indicated our mission, namely, to despise what the world loves and seeks.

—Padre Pio

Maria Pompilio was one of Padre Pio's faithful spiritual daughters. She worked as a teacher in San Giovanni Rotondo. She attended Padre Pio's Mass every morning and went to confession to him regularly. One Christmas Eve, Maria witnessed a great miracle.

Padre Pio had gone to the sacristy of the church around 8:00 p.m. to hear the men's confessions. It happened to be a very cold night. Because there was no heating in the monastery at that time, a stove had been placed in the sacristy to take the chill off.

While Padre Pio was hearing the men's confessions, Maria Pompilio and several other women stayed in the church to pray. After the confessions were over, Maria and her companions went into the sacristy to greet Padre Pio and to kiss his hand. Maria noticed that Padre Pio's hand was ice cold.

Padre Pio greeted his spiritual daughters and said to them, "May the Child Jesus make you feel his mercy and his tender love." "It is so cold tonight, Padre Pio," one of the women said. "Please speak to us for a while. Tell us more about the Infant Jesus and fill us with the warmth of his love."

Padre Pio then took his spiritual daughters to the visitors' room in the monastery. There stood a long table with enough chairs for everyone to be seated comfortably. Padre Pio spoke about the Christmas mysteries and said, "Daughters, let us meditate on the words from the Gospel of John. John, the beloved disciple, said, 'And the Word was made flesh and dwelt among us.'" Tears filled Padre Pio's eyes as he quoted the words from scripture. He paused for a moment to dry his eyes and then he reflected on the privations of Jesus's birth and infancy. He spoke of how Jesus was born in the winter, the coldest season of the year, in the depth of the night. There among the animals, he was laid in the manger. Mary and Joseph attended him lovingly while the angels in heaven rejoiced.

Suddenly Padre Pio closed his eyes and became silent. "Padre Pio has fallen asleep," one of the women whispered.

"He heard confessions all day today, and he is exhausted. Let's be very quiet and use the time to pray until he wakes up." "I do not think he is asleep," one of the other women said. "This is Christmas Eve. I believe Padre Pio is in deep communion with Jesus at this very moment. It is truly a privilege for us to be sitting here with him."

After about thirty minutes, Padre Pio opened his eyes. One of his spiritual daughters then said to him, "Padre Pio, you were silent for a long time. Since it is Christmas Eve, we were wondering if you were with the baby Jesus?" Padre Pio made no reply. Another said, "Padre Pio, please tell us what you experienced as you sat with your eyes closed." "If you promise not to say a word about it until after my death, I will tell you," Padre Pio replied. "We give you our word that we will tell no one," the women said in unison.

Padre Pio then said to the women, "The Lord permitted me to wish a happy Christmas to my brother, Michael, who is in America and also to my sister, Sister Pia, in her convent in Rome. Then Jesus showed me all of my spiritual children who have passed on to eternal life, and I saw their dwelling places in heaven." The women were deeply inspired by his words.

Before long, it was time for Padre Pio to prepare for the celebration of the Christmas midnight Mass. Softly glowing candles illuminated the little sixteenth-century church of Our Lady of Grace. When the Mass began, Padre Pio, holding a small statue of the baby Jesus in his arms, processed solemnly down the aisle toward the Christmas crib. Together with the choir, the Capuchins and the entire congregation sang Christmas carols and hymns of praise to God. All hearts seemed to glow with the fire of God's love.

After the midnight Mass, before retiring to his cell, Padre Pio spoke to his spiritual daughters for the last time that evening and said, "Tonight heaven opened, and many graces came down into your souls." Truly, they had all been blessed.

Read

While they were there, the time came for her to have her child, and she gave birth to her firstborn son. She wrapped him in swaddling clothes and laid him in a manger, because there was no room for them in the inn.

—Luke 2:6–7

Reflect

Jesus continues to love me and to draw me closer to himself. He has forgotten my sins, and I would say that he remembers only His own mercy. . . . Each morning he comes into my heart and pours out all the effusions of His goodness.

—Padre Pio

On this most holy night, let us bring ourselves into the presence of the child Jesus. Let us imagine that we are kneeling at the manger and the child Jesus is aglow with love for us.

O Night of Love!

Let Us Pray

Padre Pio, we pray you will stay close to us on this journey. We pray that we will arrive at Bethlehem with hearts full of hope, peace, joy, and love for the child Jesus!

Conclude your time of reflection and prayer with one Our Father, one Hail Mary, and one Glory Be.

Day 29

Christmas Day

May the Child Jesus be the star that guides you through the desert of your present life.

—Padre Pio

Padre Pio's Christmas Meditation

Far into the night, at the coldest time of the year, in a chilly grotto more suitable for a flock of beasts than for humans, the promised Messiah—Jesus—the Savior of mankind, comes into the world in the fullness of time.

There are none who clamor around him: only an ox and an ass lending their warmth to the newborn infant; with a humble woman, and a poor and tired man, in adoration beside him.

Nothing can be heard except the sobs and whimpers of the infant God. And by means of his crying and weeping he offers to the Divine justice the first ransom for our redemption.

He had been expected for forty centuries; with longing sighs the ancient Fathers had implored his arrival. The sacred scriptures clearly prophesy the time and the place of his birth, and yet the world is silent, and no one seems aware of the great event. Only some shepherds, who had been busy watching over their sheep in the meadows, come to visit him. Heavenly visitors had alerted them to the wondrous event, inviting them to approach his cave.

So plentiful, O Christians, are the lessons that shine forth from the grotto of Bethlehem! Oh, how our hearts should be on fire with love for the one who with such tenderness was made flesh for our sakes! Oh, how we should burn with desire to lead the whole world to this lowly cave, refuge of the King of kings, greater than any worldly palace, because it is the throne and dwelling place of God! Let us ask this Divine child to clothe us with humility, because only by means of this virtue can we taste the fullness of this mystery of Divine tenderness.

Glittering were the palaces of the proud Hebrews. Yet, the Light of the world did not appear in one of them. Ostentatious with worldly grandeur, swimming in gold and in delights, were the great ones of the Hebrew nation; filled with vain knowledge and pride were the priests of the sanctuary. In opposition to the true meaning of Divine revelation, they awaited an officious Savior who would come into the world with human renown and power.

But God, always ready to confound the wisdom of the world, shatters their plans. Contrary to the expectations of those lacking in Divine wisdom, he appears among us in the greatest abjection, renouncing even birth in St. Joseph's humble home, denying himself a modest abode among relatives and friends in a city of Palestine. Refused lodging among men, he seeks refuge and comfort among mere animals, choosing their habitation as the place of his birth, allowing their breath to give warmth to his tender body. He permits simple and rustic shepherds to be the first to pay their respects to him, after he himself informed them, by means of his angels, of the wonderful mystery.

Oh, wisdom and power of God, we are constrained to exclaim—enraptured along with your Apostle—how incomprehensible are your judgments and unsearchable your ways! Poverty, humility, abjection, contempt all surround the Word made flesh. But we, out of the darkness that envelops the incarnate Word, understand one thing, hear one voice, perceive one sublime truth: you have done everything out of love, you invite us to nothing else but love, speak of nothing except love, give us naught except proofs of love.

The heavenly babe suffers and cries in the crib so that for us suffering would be sweet, meritorious and accepted. He deprives himself of everything, in order that we may learn from him the renunciation of worldly goods and comforts. He is satisfied with humble and poor adorers, to encourage us to love poverty, and to prefer the company of the little and simple rather than the great ones of the world.

This celestial child, all meekness and sweetness, wishes to impress in our hearts by his example these sublime virtues, so that from a world that is torn and devastated an era of peace and love may spring forth. Even from the moment of his birth he reveals to us our mission, which is to scorn that which the world loves and seeks.

Oh, let us prostrate ourselves before the manger, and along with the great St. Jerome, who was enflamed with the love of the infant Jesus, let us offer him all our hearts without reserve. Let us promise to follow the precepts which come to us from the grotto of Bethlehem, which teach us that everything here below is vanity of vanities, nothing but vanity.[11]

Read

But you, Bethlehem-Ephrathah least among the clans of Judah, From you shall come forth for me one who is to be ruler in Israel; Whose origin is from of old, from ancient times.

—Micah 5:2

Reflect

In the spiritual life, the more you run the less you get tired; moreover, peace, the preclude to eternal joy, will come upon us, and we shall be happy and strong according to the extent that we live in this study of making Jesus live in us, and of mortifying ourselves.

—Padre Pio

Let us comfort the child Jesus and dry his tears with our hearts of love.

O come, let us adore him!

Let Us Pray

Padre Pio, we pray you will stay close to us on this journey. We pray that we will arrive at Bethlehem with hearts full of hope, peace, joy, and love for the child Jesus!

Conclude your time of reflection and prayer with one Our Father, one Hail Mary, and one Glory Be.

Acknowledgments and Bibliography

Most of the stories shared in this book come from Ray Ewen's stories of Padre Pio and my memory.

Thanks to Diane Allen, who compiled many of the stories shared in this book from both the Capuchins and the original recipients of Padre Pio's miracles on her website, Padre Pio Devotions (padrepiodevotions.org). Her records were invaluable to me as I wrote this book and fact-checked details of the stories.

Padre Pio's quotes at the beginning of each story were from various sites and books. These quotes can be found in the Capuchin archives in San Giovanni Rotundo.

Thank you to the National Centre for Padre Pio (padrepio.org) for giving me permission to use Vera Calandra's story.

Thank you to the Padre Pio Foundation of America for their permission to share stories from *Mary's House* by Dorothy M. Gaudiose and the story of Joe Spada shared on "Day 25: A Visit from Padre Pio."

Thank you to Frank M. Rega for permission to use his translation of Padre Pio's Christmas Meditation, which came from Padre Pio's handwritten notebooks. Rega is the author of *Amazing Miracles of Padre Pio: And the Stories Behind Them.*

Books

Allegri, Renzo. *Padre Pio: Man of Hope*. Cincinnati, OH: Servant, 2000.

Cataneo, Pascal. *Padre Pio: Glimpse into the Miraculous*. Boston: Pauline Books and Media, 1991.

Gaudiose, Dorothy M. *Mary's House: Mary Pyle: Under the Spiritual Guidance of Padre Pio*. Staten Island, NY: Alba House, 1992.

Padre Pio of Pietrelcina. *Letters*. Vol. 1, *Correspondence with His Spiritual Directors (1910–1922)*. San Giovanni Rotondo, Italy: Our Lady of Grace Capuchin Friary, 1980.

———. *Letters*. Vol. 2, *Correspondence with Raffaelina Cerase, Noblewoman (1914–1915)*. San Giovanni Rotondo, Italy: Our Lady of Grace Capuchin Friary, 1997.

———. *Letters*. Vol. 3, *Correspondence with His Spiritual Daughters (1915–1923)*. San Giovanni Rotondo, Italy: Our Lady of Grace Capuchin Friary, 1984.

Websites

Testimonies

Padre Pio Devotions. padrepiodevotions.org.

Most Holy Family Monastery. vaticancatholic.com.

rezoelrosario.com. corevans.com.

ACKNOWLEDGMENTS

Padre Pio Foundation of America. padrepio.com.
National Centre for Padre Pio. padrepio.org.
Padre Pio Devotions. padrepiodevotions.com.
Voce di Padre Pio. vocedipadrepio.com.

Appendix I

Additional Resources

Padre Pio Foundation of America

The Padre Pio Foundation of America (PPFOA) began in 1977. It is a nonprofit dedicated to carrying out the legacy of Padre Pio. Padre Pio's mission in life was to help the needy and the suffering. With the support of thousands of benefactors, Padre Pio's loving touch can be felt around the world.

The PPFOA works with missionary priests and sisters in the United States and in other countries, including Mexico, Haiti, Vietnam, the Philippines, Peru, and Chad. They provide assistance such as food, shelter, and medicine along with spiritual assistance by building a chapel for communities that have no place to worship.

The PPFOA also supports Padre Pio's life work, the hospital he called La Casa Sollievo della Sofferenza, the Home for the Relief of Suffering. He loved his friary in San Giovanni Rotondo and his hometown of Pietrelcina, and PPFOA continues to assist them as pilgrimage sites.

The PPFOA also takes great pride in sharing Padre Pio's life, spirituality, teachings, and special gifts given to him by God. They continuously assist all those who seek his intercession.

For more information, you can visit www.padrepio. com, Facebook at the Padre Pio Foundation of America, or Instagram @padrepiofoundation.

To schedule a pilgrimage to the Padre Pio Foundation of America or to be part of one of their pilgrimages in the footsteps of Padre Pio, please visit www.padrepio.com.

Padre Pio Foundation of America
463 Main Street
Cromwell, CT 06416
Phone: (860) 635-4996
Fax: (860) 635-7746
Email: padrepio@padrepio.com

National Centre for Padre Pio

The goal of the National Centre for Padre Pio, Inc., is to lead souls to God through the example of Padre Pio, the first priest in history to bear the stigmata, the wounds of Christ.

Based on the precepts of Franciscan spirituality as demonstrated by the Seraphic Father, St. Francis of Assisi, Padre Pio's own spirituality was a lifelong practice of love of God as manifested through love of neighbor. Through his mission on the altar and in the confessional, particularly as a spiritual teacher second to none, Padre Pio continued the work of redemption begun by Christ.

In thanksgiving to God for this unique gift of Padre Pio in our lives, the center humbly strives to continue the salvific mission of Padre Pio. They offer to all, regardless of race, creed, or color, a place of refuge and revitalization where the sacraments are readily available in the Franciscan spirit of love and peace.

In this place of refuge, they endeavor to educate and promote education in the teachings and spirituality of Padre Pio through speeches, seminars, workshops, retreats, and pilgrimages.

The center publishes, distributes, composes, and produces books, magazines, music, and films about the life, work, and spirituality of Padre Pio both in the United States and throughout the world.

To schedule a pilgrimage, visit www.padrepio.org.

National Centre for Padre Pio
111 Barto Road
Barto, PA 19504
Phone: (610) 845-3000
Website: www.padrepio.org
Email: info@padrepio.org
Facebook: www.facebook.com/PadrePioInc

Padre Pio Devotions

Padre Pio Devotions is a website devoted to Padre Pio. Its creator, Diane Allen, keeps followers updated on all that is going on in the world of Padre Pio.

Padre Pio said, "Unite yourself to my prayers." At Padre Pio Devotions, you will find the prayers of Padre Pio, including the Novena to the Sacred Heart of Jesus, which he prayed every day. You can also pray the Divine Office with Morning Prayer (Lauds), Evening Prayer (Vespers), and Night Prayer (Compline).

Padre Pio Devotions publications include *Pray, Hope, and Don't Worry: True Stories of Padre Pio Book I* and *Pray, Hope, and Don't Worry: True Stories of Padre Pio Book II* as well as *Daily Reflection: 365 Reflections from the Saints and Other Holy Men and Women of God*—all written by Diane Allen.

In the Testimony section, you can read some of the amazing miracles that occurred through the intercession of Padre Pio. You can find a few of these stories in this book. One of the stories, "Day 14: Stay with Me Lord," was told by Deacon Ron Allen, Diane's husband.

Visit the Archives to read the Padre Pio newsletter, filled with inspirational stories about St. Pio of Pietrelcina and those whose lives he touched.

Visit Padre Pio Devotions online at https://padrepiodevotions.org.

Facebook: www.facebook.com/PadrePioDevotions

Instagram: www.instagram.com/saint_pio_of_pietrelcina

Voce di Padre Pio Foundation

"Voce di Padre Pio" Foundation is managed by Capuchin Friars of San Giovanni Rotondo and spreads the message and life of Padre Pio in the world. On May 11, 2006, Voce di Padre Pio was established as the "operational arm" for the creation of cultural, publishing, and evangelization activities of the Religious Province of Sant'Angelo and Padre Pio of the Capuchin Friars from which it has been promoted.

The magazine *Voce di Padre Pio* was founded in July 1970, by the Capuchin Friars of the Sant'Angleo, Foggia Province, "to safeguard Padre Pio's integrity," "to gather the authentic aspects of his spirituality drawn from his life and teaching," "to illustrate the charitable and religious movement which has formed and continues to develop around him," "to describe the life of the shrine of Our Lady of Grace, where Padre Pio lived and worked," "to give news of those heavenly graces and favors which are attributed to his intercession," and "to give information on the Cause of Beatification and Canonization."

At present the magazine is printed in Italian, English, French, German, and Spanish. Visit www.vocedipadrepio.com to learn more.

"Voce di Padre Pio" Foundation/Tele Radio Padre Pio is the broadcasting station of the Capuchin Friars of the Religious Province of Sant'Angelo and Padre Pio.

It broadcasts from San Giovanni Rotondo. It is a Catholic station that aims to spread the message of the Gospel through the teachings and experiences of St. Pio of Pietrelcina.

The station broadcasts its signal over the air in almost all of Puglia and has entered into a partnership agreement with the national broadcasting station Padre Pio TV of the association that also broadcasts via satellite in Europe and the Mediterranean area.

The programming schedule is based on the celebrations that take place in the sacred places of San Giovanni Rotondo. But there are also news programs, current affairs, culture, catechesis, and reflections on the writings and life example of Padre Pio. The Angelus and the General Audience of His Holiness Pope Francis are broadcast Sundays and Wednesdays. The broadcasting of live images from the crypt is widely followed. To view live broadcasts, go to www.teleradiopadrepio.it.

The "Padre Pio" Reading Room was established in May 1990. It specializes in the spirituality and life of Padre Pio; the need and request came from Padre Pio's followers. Pilgrims and tourists wanted a reading center where they could learn more about the life and spirituality of St. Pio of Pietrelcina.

The room has a nearly complete collection of all that has been written about the stigmatized monk from 1919 to the present day.

Appendix II

Prayers of Padre Pio

Stay with Me Lord

Padre Pio prayed this prayer after Communion.

Stay with me, Lord, for it is necessary to have you present
    so that I do not forget you.
You know how easily I abandon you.
Stay with me, Lord, because I am weak and I need your
    strength, that I may not fall so often.
Stay with me, Lord, for you are my life, and without you,
    I am without meaning and hope.
Stay with me, Lord, for you are my light, and without you,
    I am in darkness.
Stay with me, Lord, to show me your will.
Stay with me, Lord, so that I can hear your voice and
    follow you.
Stay with me, Lord, for I desire to love you ever more, and
    to be in your company always.
Stay with me, Lord, if you wish me to be faithful to you.
Stay with me, Lord, for as poor as my soul is, I wish it to
    be a place of consolation for you, a dwelling of
    your love.

Stay with me, Jesus, for it is getting late; the days are coming to a close, and life is passing. Death, judgment, eternity are drawing near. It is necessary to renew my strength, so that I will not stop along the way and for that, I need you.

It is getting late and death approaches. I fear the darkness, the temptations, the dryness, the cross, the sorrows.

O how I need you, my Jesus, in this night of exile!

Stay with me, Jesus, because in the darkness of life, with all its dangers, I need you.

Help me to recognize you as your disciples did at the breaking of the bread,

so that the Eucharistic Communion be the Light which disperses the darkness,

the power which sustains me, the unique joy of my heart.

Stay with me, Lord, because at the hour of my death I want to be one with you,

and if not by communion, at least by your grace and love.

Stay with me, Jesus, I do not ask for divine consolations because I do not deserve them,

but I only ask for the gift of your presence. Oh yes, I ask this of you!

Stay with me, Lord, for I seek you alone, your Love, your Grace, your Will, your Heart, your Spirit, because I love you and I ask no other reward but to love you more and more with a strong and active love.

Grant that I may love you with all my heart while on earth, so that I can continue to love you perfectly throughout all eternity, dear Jesus. Amen!

Efficacious Novena to the Sacred Heart of Jesus

Padre Pio said this novena every day.

O my Jesus, you have said: "Truly I say to you, ask and it will be given you, seek and you will find, knock and it will be opened to you." Behold I knock, I seek and ask for the grace of *[insert your intention]*.

Our Father . . . Hail Mary . . . Glory be to the Father . . . Sacred Heart of Jesus, I place all my trust in you.

O my Jesus, you have said: "Truly I say to you, if you ask any thing of the Father in my name, he will give it to you." Behold, in your name, I ask the Father for the grace of *[insert your intention]*.

Our Father . . . Hail Mary . . . Glory be to the Father . . . Sacred Heart of Jesus, I place all my trust in you.

O my Jesus, you have said: "Truly I say to you, heaven and earth will pass away but my words will not pass away." Encouraged by your infallible words I now ask for the grace of *[insert your intention]*.

Our Father . . . Hail Mary . . . Glory be to the Father . . . Sacred Heart of Jesus, I place all my trust in you.

O Sacred Heart of Jesus, for whom it is impossible not to have compassion on the afflicted, have pity on us miserable sinners and grant us the grace which we ask of you, through the Sorrowful and Immaculate Heart of Mary, your tender mother and ours.

Hail, Holy Queen, Mother of Mercy, our life, our sweetness and our hope! To thee do we cry, poor banished children of Eve. To thee do we send up our sighs, mourning and weeping in this valley of tears! Turn, then, O most gracious Advocate, thine eyes of mercy toward us, and after this, our exile, show unto us the blessed fruit of thy womb, Jesus. O clement, O loving, O sweet Virgin Mary.

St. Joseph, foster father of Jesus, pray for us.

Prayer to St. Michael the Archangel

Padre Pio had a great lifelong devotion to St. Michael, the archangel, and he encouraged everyone to pray to him every day.

St. Michael the Archangel,
defend us in battle.
Be our protection against the wickedness and snares of the Devil.
May God rebuke him, we humbly pray,
and do thou,
O Prince of the heavenly hosts,
by the power of God,
cast into hell Satan,
and all the evil spirits,
who roam about the world
seeking the ruin of souls. Amen.

NOTES

1. Padre Pio of Pietrelcina, *Letters: Correspondence with His Spiritual Directors (1910–1922)*, vol. 1, ed. Mariano Di Vito (San Giovanni Rotondo, Italy: Edfizioi Press, 1985).

2. Padre Pio, *Letters: Correspondence with His Spiritual Directors.*

3. Padre Pio, *Letters: Correspondence with His Spiritual Directors.*

4. Padre Pio, *Letters: Correspondence with His Spiritual Directors.*

5. Padre Pio, *Letters: Correspondence with His Spiritual Directors.*

6. Padre Pio of Pietrelcina, *Letters: Correspondence with Raffaelina Cearse, Noblewoman (1914–1915)*, vol. 2, ed. Mariano Di Vito (San Giovanni Rotondo, Italy: Edfizioi Press, 1987).

7. Padre Pio, *Letters: Correspondence with His Spiritual Directors.*

8. Dorothy M. Gaudoise, *Mary's House: Mary Pyle: Under the Spiritual Guidance of Padre Pio* (Staten Island, NY: Alba House, 1992).

9. Gaudoise, *Mary's House.*

10. Padre Pio of Pietrelcina, *Letters: Correspondence with His Spiritual Directors.*

11. This meditation was taken from Padre Pio's handwritten notebooks and was translated by Frank M. Rega. Used with permission.

Susan De Bartoli is a pilgrimage tour operator and owner of Little Flower Tours & Travel. She is helping with the Cause for Canonization of Mary Pyle, assistant to Padre Pio.

De Bartoli also writes a weekly column, called "Through the Fields of My Mind," for an online newsletter about the Italian pop music trio Il Volo that reaches at least 500,000 fans in Italy and the United States.

She attended Brooklyn College. De Bartoli is a Lady Commander of the Equestrian Order of the Holy Sepulchre of Jerusalem. She lives in the New York area.